Aircraft Accident Report

**In-Flight Electrical System Failure
and Loss of Control
Jet Express Services
Raytheon (Beechcraft) Super King Air 200,
N81PF
Near Strasburg, Colorado
January 27, 2001**

NTSB/AAR-03/01
PB2003-910401
Notation 7358A
Adopted January 15, 2003

National Transportation Safety Board
490 L'Enfant Plaza, S.W.
Washington, D.C. 20594

National Transportation Safety Board. 2003. *In-Flight Electrical System Failure and Loss of Control, Jet Express Services, Raytheon (Beechcraft) Super King Air 200, N81PF, Near Strasburg, Colorado, January 27, 2001.* Aircraft Accident Report NTSB/AAR-03/01. Washington, DC.

Abstract: This report explains the accident involving a Jet Express Services Raytheon (Beechcraft) Super King Air 200 airplane, which crashed near Strasburg, Colorado. The safety issue discussed in this report is the lack of oversight for athletic team and other college- and university-sponsored travel. A safety recommendation concerning this issue is addressed to the National Collegiate Athletic Association, the National Association of Intercollegiate Athletics, and the American Council on Education.

Contents

Figures

Abbreviations

a.c.	alternating current
AC	advisory circular
AIRMET	airmen's meteorological information
ARTCC	air route traffic control center
ASOS	automated surface observing system
ASR-9	airport surveillance radar-9
ATC	air traffic control
ATCT	air traffic control tower
ATIS	automatic terminal information service
AWOS	automated weather observing system
BJC	Jefferson County Airport
C	Celsius
CFR	*Code of Federal Regulations*
d.c.	direct current
FAA	Federal Aviation Administration
FAR	Federal Aviation Regulation
Hg	mercury
HSI	horizontal situation indicator
Hz	Hertz
IFR	instrument flight rules
ILS	instrument landing system
IMC	instrument meteorological conditions
nm	nautical mile
NWS	National Weather Service

OSU	Oklahoma State University
PennDOT	Pennsylvania Department of Transportation
PIC	pilot-in-command
PWA	Wiley Post Airport
RMI	radio magnetic indicator
SIGMET	significant meteorological information
S/N	serial number
SWO	Stillwater Regional Airport
TRACON	terminal radar approach control
VFR	visual flight rules
WSR-88D	Weather Surveillance Radar 1988 Doppler

Executive Summary

On January 27, 2001, about 1737 mountain standard time, a Raytheon (Beechcraft) Super King Air 200, N81PF, owned by North Bay Charter, LLC, and operated by Jet Express Services, crashed into rolling terrain near Strasburg, Colorado. The flight was operating on an instrument flight rules flight plan under 14 *Code of Federal Regulations* Part 91. The flight departed about 1718 from Jefferson County Airport, Broomfield, Colorado, with two pilots and eight passengers aboard. N81PF was one of three airplanes transporting members of the Oklahoma State University basketball team and associated team personnel to Stillwater Regional Airport, Stillwater, Oklahoma, after a game at the University of Colorado at Boulder that afternoon. All 10 occupants aboard N81PF were killed, and the airplane was destroyed by impact forces and a postcrash fire. Instrument meteorological conditions prevailed at the time of the accident.

The National Transportation Safety Board determines that the probable cause of this accident was the pilot's spatial disorientation resulting from his failure to maintain positive manual control of the airplane with the available flight instrumentation. Contributing to the cause of the accident was the loss of a.c. electrical power during instrument meteorological conditions.

The safety issue discussed in this report is the lack of oversight for athletic team and other college- and university-sponsored travel. A safety recommendation concerning this issue is addressed to the National Collegiate Athletic Association, the National Association of Intercollegiate Athletics, and the American Council on Education.

1.   Factual Information

1.1   History of Flight

On January 27, 2001, about 1737 mountain standard time,[1] a Raytheon (Beechcraft) Super King Air 200,[2] N81PF, owned by North Bay Charter, LLC, and operated by Jet Express Services, crashed into rolling terrain near Strasburg, Colorado. The flight was operating on an instrument flight rules (IFR) flight plan under 14 *Code of Federal Regulations* (CFR) Part 91. The flight departed about 1718 from Jefferson County Airport (BJC), Broomfield, Colorado, with two pilots and eight passengers aboard. The pilot who occupied the left seat in the cockpit was solely responsible for the flight.[3] The pilot who occupied the right seat in the cockpit, referred to in this report as the "second pilot," was not a required flight crewmember. N81PF was one of three airplanes[4] transporting members of the Oklahoma State University (OSU) basketball team and associated team personnel to Stillwater Regional Airport (SWO), Stillwater, Oklahoma, after a game at the University of Colorado at Boulder that afternoon. All 10 occupants aboard N81PF were killed, and the airplane was destroyed by impact forces and a postcrash fire. Instrument meteorological conditions (IMC) prevailed at the time of the accident.

On the day before the accident, the pilots departed Wiley Post Airport (PWA), near Oklahoma City, Oklahoma, for a positioning flight to SWO.[5] At SWO, members of the OSU basketball team and associated team personnel boarded the airplane, which then continued to BJC. According to ATC records, N81PF made its first radio contact with the Kansas City ARTCC about 1449 (1549 central standard time) and its last radio contact with the Denver Terminal Radar Approach Control (TRACON) about 1652. Records from Stevens Aviation, a fixed-base operator at BJC, indicated that the airplane landed at 1700 and was placed in a hangar overnight.

ATC records indicated that the pilot contacted the Denver Automated Flight Service Station about 1100 on the day of the accident to obtain a weather briefing and file IFR flight plans for the return trips to SWO and PWA. The weather briefing included a

---

[1] Unless otherwise indicated, all times are mountain standard time, based on a 24-hour clock. The times contained in this report are approximations based on air traffic control (ATC) radar data and transcript information.

[2] Raytheon Aircraft Company acquired Beech Aircraft Corporation in February 1980.

[3] King Air operations under 14 CFR Part 91 require only one pilot.

[4] The other two airplanes were a Learjet 60, N250FX, and a Cessna Citation 650, N77LX. These flights were operating under 14 CFR Part 91.

[5] Precise departure and arrival information could not be determined. According to ATC information, the pilot maintained radio contact with the Kansas City Air Route Traffic Control Center (ARTCC) between 1357 and 1407 (1457 and 1507 central standard time). The distance between the two airports is about 47 nautical miles (nm), and the entire flight was estimated to have taken no more than 25 minutes.

general synopsis of the weather situation for the proposed flights, AIRMET [airmen's meteorological information][6] flight advisories for occasional moderate icing and occasional moderate turbulence, forecast airport conditions, winds and temperatures aloft, and notices to airmen in effect. A Stevens Aviation ramp worker at BJC stated that the airplane was pulled outside from its overnight hangar between 1115 and 1130 on the day of the accident. The ramp worker also stated that the pilots arrived at the airport sometime after 1300. The pilot requested that the airplane be returned to a hangar until after the passengers boarded. According to the ramp worker, the airplane was subsequently returned to another hangar.[7] The pilots left the airport to attend at least the first half of the basketball game, which began at 1400.

According to ATC records, the pilot contacted BJC ground control about 1631 to obtain an IFR clearance to SWO, and the ground controller issued the clearance as filed. The Stevens Aviation ramp worker indicated that the passengers arrived at BJC at 1700. After the passengers boarded the airplane, it was towed from the hangar.[8] About 1712, the pilot contacted ground control to request taxi instructions, indicating that he had received automatic terminal information service (ATIS) information Quebec.[9] Because ATIS information Romeo[10] was current at the time, the ground controller issued the new weather information along with the taxi clearance to runway 29R.

About 1717:15, the pilot of N81PF reported that the airplane was ready to depart from runway 29R. The ground controller instructed the pilot to hold short of the runway while awaiting an IFR release. The ground controller then contacted the Denver TRACON for an IFR release, which was issued about 1717:38. The BJC local controller cleared N81PF for takeoff about 1717:49 and instructed the airplane to turn right to a 040° heading. About 1719:47, the local controller instructed the pilot to contact the Denver TRACON.

---

[6] An AIRMET is an in-flight weather advisory issued by the National Weather Service (NWS) Aviation Weather Center in Kansas City, Missouri. An AIRMET advisory indicates weather that may be hazardous to single-engine and other light aircraft and visual flight rules (VFR) pilots. Operators of large aircraft may also be concerned with the information included in an AIRMET.

[7] The ramp worker indicated that the airplane was refueled with 260 gallons of Jet A fuel before returning to the hangar. Each King Air 200 main fuel tank has a 191-gallon capacity, and each auxiliary fuel tank has a 40-gallon capacity. Fuel samples from the refueling truck and the accident airplane's right wing fuel tank were analyzed, and both samples were found to conform to specifications.

[8] The Stevens Aviation ramp worker indicated that the airplane was dry when it was towed from the hangar and that the temperature in the hangar was about 60° to 65°. The ramp worker also indicated that the airplane was airborne about 5 to 7 minutes after it had been towed from the hangar. Further, the ramp worker stated that the airplane was loaded with "small overnight bags and a few duffel bags."

[9] ATIS information Quebec was issued at 1545 and stated that the wind was calm, visibility was 1 mile in light snow, sky condition was an indefinite ceiling of 200 feet, temperature was -3° Celsius (C), dew point was -5° C, altimeter setting was 29.99 inches of mercury (Hg), and the instrument landing system (ILS) runway 29R approach was in use.

[10] ATIS information Romeo was issued at 1652 and stated that the wind was variable at 3 knots, visibility was 1 mile in light snow, sky condition was an indefinite ceiling of 200 feet, temperature was -4° C, dew point was -5° C, altimeter setting was 30.00 inches of Hg, and the ILS runway 29R approach was in use.

About 1719:55, the pilot contacted the Denver Departure Radar Four position and reported that he was climbing through 6,500 feet[11] to 8,000 feet. Afterward, the departure controller issued a clearance for the airplane to climb to 12,000 feet and then instructed the pilot to fly the airplane on a 060° heading. About 1722:09, the controller instructed the pilot to proceed to the EPKEE intersection, join the Garden City transition, and climb to 23,000 feet. The pilot acknowledged these instructions.

About 1724:07, the departure controller instructed the pilot to fly the airplane on a 110° heading, and the pilot acknowledged this instruction. About 1725:53, the controller instructed the pilot to contact the Satellite Radar Two controller. The pilot contacted the Satellite Radar Two controller about 1726:06, reporting out of 16,300 feet and climbing to 23,000 feet. The controller asked the pilot whether he was flying directly to the EPKEE intersection, and the pilot responded that he had been proceeding to the intersection but had been assigned a heading of 110°. About 1726:20, the controller cleared the airplane to proceed directly to the EPKEE intersection. About 1726:27, the pilot stated that he was going directly to the EPKEE intersection and that he needed to make about a 3° left turn. The controller did not receive any further transmissions from the pilot.

Mode C information from the airplane's transponder[12] indicated that the airplane reached its cruising altitude of 23,000 feet about 1732:35. According to ATC radar data, the airplane's climb through this altitude was normal, and its airspeeds had been steady. The last mode C transponder return occurred about 1735:44, when the airplane was at an altitude of 23,200 feet. Radar data indicated that the airplane started to deviate from its heading and to turn to the right by about 1736:26 (about 42 seconds after mode C information was lost).

Mode A information from the transponder remained available until about 1737:12.[13] Within the next 5 to 8 seconds (sometime between 1737:17 and 1737:20), the airplane impacted rolling terrain at an elevation of 5,223 feet. The accident occurred at 39° 44.822 minutes north latitude and 104° 15.037 minutes west longitude after official sunset but before the end of evening civil twilight.[14] Figure 1 shows the airplane's flight track, according to ATC radar data, for the last 2 minutes of the accident flight.

---

[11] All altitudes in this report are mean sea level.

[12] A transponder transmits an airplane's identification and altitude information in response to interrogation signals received from ground-based radar equipment. Mode C information, if available, provides the airplane's altitude in 100-foot increments.

[13] Mode A information provides the airplane's four-digit beacon (identification) code. Ground-based radar equipment observes this information and calculates the airplane's direction (azimuth) and distance from the radar antenna. During the final minute of the flight, two beacon returns were transmitted but were not received because of the airplane's orientation (that is, the airplane's antenna was not in the line of sight of the ground-based radar equipment).

[14] On the day of the accident, official sunset for the Denver, Colorado, area occurred at 1716, and evening civil twilight for the area ended at 1744. (Title 14 CFR Part 1.1 states that night begins after the end of evening civil twilight.) At the time of the accident, the sun was -4.7° below the horizon, and the moon was 36° above the horizon with 16 percent illumination.

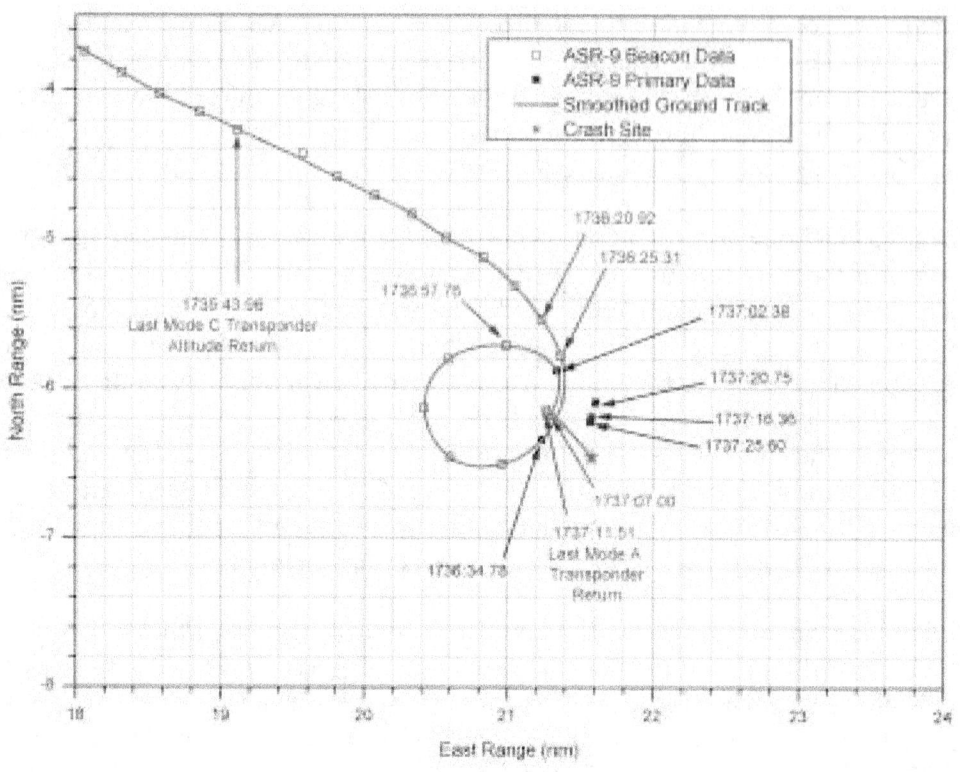

Note: Airport surveillance radar-9 (ASR-9) primary data are reflected radio signals. ASR-9 primary data returns were received until about 1737:26, about 14 seconds after the last mode A (beacon data) return. The distances shown are relative to the ASR-9 radar site at Denver International Airport.

Figure 1. Radar data for the last 2 minutes of the accident flight.

1.2 Injuries to Persons

Table 1. Injury chart.

Injuries	Flight Crew	Cabin Crew	Passengers	Other	Total
Fatal	2	0	8	0	10
Serious	0	0	0	0	0
Minor	0	0	0	0	0
None	0	0	0	0	0
Total	2	0	8	0	10

1.3 Damage to Airplane

The airplane was destroyed by impact forces and a postcrash fire.

1.4 Other Damage

No other damage was reported.

1.5 Personnel Information

1.5.1 The Pilot

The pilot, age 55, held a Federal Aviation Administration (FAA) airline transport pilot certificate. He also held an FAA second-class medical certificate dated January 25, 2001, with a limitation that required lenses to correct for near and distant vision. The pilot received his private pilot's license in December 1969 and his commercial pilot's license in January 1971. He received a Cessna 500 type rating in March 1989 and a Learjet type rating in July 1994. (A type rating is not required for the King Air 200.) He was also a certified flight instructor.

According to the pilot's logbook, he had accumulated 5,117 hours total flying time, including 3,650 hours as a multiengine pilot-in-command (PIC) and 2,520 hours in King Air airplanes (767 hours of which were as a King Air 200 PIC). He had flown approximately 51, 13, and 0.4[15] hours in the 90 days, 30 days, and 24 hours, respectively, before the accident. According to documents from SIMCOM Training Center of Scottsdale, Arizona, the pilot's last recurrent ground and simulator training occurred on April 20 and 21, 2000. He satisfactorily completed a recurrent training course on the King Air 200 with King Air C90B differences. He also satisfactorily completed an instrument proficiency check, as required by Federal Aviation Regulation (FAR) 61.57, "Recent Flight Experience: Pilot in Command," and met biennial flight review requirements by completing a pilot proficiency program, in accordance with FAA Advisory Circular (AC) 61.91, "Pilot Proficiency Award Program."[16] In addition, a search of the National Driver Register database indicated no record of driver's license suspension or revocation.

The pilot's family described his health as "good" and indicated that he did not smoke and that he consumed alcoholic beverages "socially in moderation." The pilot's family also indicated that no changes in his health or in his personal, professional, or

---

[15] This figure reflects the estimated duration of the accident flight. The flight from SWO to BJC on the day before the accident is not included in this figure because the airplane had landed at 1700.

[16] SIMCOM documents also indicated that, from January 28 to 30, 1999, the pilot completed ground and simulator training for the King Air 200 and differences training for the King Air C90B. In addition, the pilot's logbook indicated that, from July 21 to 23, 1997, he completed King Air 200 training at Flight Safety International in Wichita, Kansas.

financial situation had occurred in the year before the accident. In addition, the pilot's family indicated that he did not suffer from any sleep disorders.

According to the pilot's family, on January 24, 2001, he awoke about 0630 central standard time and went to work. (He was a partner in an accounting firm in Oklahoma City.) Afterward, he went to PWA and then home, where he spent the rest of the evening. He went to sleep about 2300 central standard time. On January 25, 2001, the pilot awoke about 0630 central standard time, went to work in the morning, received his FAA medical examination in the afternoon, went back to work, stopped by PWA, arrived home between 1800 and 1900 central standard time, and went to sleep about 2300 central standard time. On January 26, 2001, the pilot awoke about 0630 central standard time and went to work. He left work about 1200 central standard time to go to PWA to prepare for the flights to SWO and BJC. Records from a hotel in Boulder indicated that the pilot checked in, along with the second pilot, about 1730 on January 26th.

1.5.2 The Second Pilot

The second pilot, age 30, held an FAA first-class medical certificate dated January 27, 2000, with no limitations. The second pilot received his private pilot's license in June 1996, his IFR rating in February 1997, and his commercial pilot's license in May 1997. He was also a certified flight instructor.

According to the second pilot's logbook, he had accumulated 1,828 hours total flying time, including 1,218 hours as a multiengine pilot. He had flown approximately 87, 17, and 0.4 hours in the 90 days, 30 days, and 24 hours, respectively, before the accident. The second pilot's logbook also indicated that he completed an instrument proficiency check on May 14, 1999, as required by FAR 61.57, and that he completed a flight review on October 7, 1999, in accordance with FAR 61.56, "Flight Review." The second pilot's logbook further indicated that he had flown the accident airplane four times in the 90 days before the accident, logging 10.4 hours as PIC. A search of the National Driver Register database indicated no record of driver's license suspension or revocation.

A pilot who knew the second pilot since May 2000 and flew with him a few times each week stated that the second pilot wanted to work for an airline and was logging flight time as fast as he could. The pilot indicated that the second pilot flew with the accident pilot once or twice per month. The second pilot had not received any formal training on King Air airplanes.

The second pilot was not married and had no children. The pilot who knew the second pilot stated that he did not seem to have any personal or financial problems. On January 24, 2001, the second pilot flew with that pilot to various destinations in Texas, accumulating about 6 hours of flight time in a King Air C90B. The second pilot's activities on January 25, 2001, and on the morning of January 26, 2001, are unknown.

1.6 Airplane Information

The accident airplane, serial number (S/N) BB-158, was manufactured in 1976. The airplane was equipped with a Sperry three-axis autopilot. The airplane was also equipped with Pratt & Whitney Canada PT6A-41 turbopropeller engines and Hartzell model HC-B3TN-3C three-bladed, constant-speed propellers. The time since new for the No. 1 (left) engine, S/N PC-E 80339, was about 8,517 hours; the time since new for the No. 2 (right) engine, S/N PC-E 80292, was about 8,283 hours; and the time since overhaul for both engines was about 2,551 hours. The time since new and the time since overhaul for the No. 1 (left) propeller, S/N BUA-21161, were estimated to be 8,261 and 476 hours, respectively. The time since new and the time since overhaul for the No. 2 (right) propeller, S/N BU-6844, were estimated to be 8,737 and 1,244 hours, respectively. (All of the engine and propeller times are based on the airplane's total flying time, which was last recorded during airplane maintenance that was performed on December 8, 2000. The maintenance work order indicated that the airplane had accumulated about 8,737 hours.)[17]

The accident airplane's last weight and balance were calculated on October 18, 1999. The airplane's empty weight was about 8,048 pounds, and its center of gravity location was 185.48 inches aft of datum. On the basis of these and other calculations provided by Raytheon, at takeoff the airplane was calculated to be within its center of gravity limits but about 314 pounds overweight. (A weight and balance form for the accident flight was not recovered.)

1.6.1 Electrical System

The airplane had a 28-volt d.c. electrical system. The system uses one 34-ampere-hour, air-cooled, 20-cell, nickel-cadmium battery and two interconnected 230-ampere generators (left and right) to supply d.c. electrical power to the airplane. The battery routes power to its main bus through the battery relay. The generators route power to their main buses, including the No. 1 (left) and No. 2 (right) avionics buses, which power the communications radios. A powered battery bus would operate certain essential equipment, including ambient cockpit and instrument panel lighting, in an emergency.

The bus system includes four sub-buses that are dual-fed (that is, they receive power from either generator's main bus). All electrical loads are divided among the sub-buses, and loads with duplicate functions are connected to different sub-buses. Among the loads connected to the sub-buses are the No. 1 (left) and No. 2 (right) 600-volt static inverters, each of which converts d.c. power to a.c. power. Each inverter provides 400-Hertz (Hz),[18] 115 volts a.c. to the avionics equipment and 400-Hz, 26 volts a.c. to the engine instrument panel, but only one inverter can be engaged at a time. The inverter select switch, located on a panel below the instrument panel and to the left of the control wheel on the pilot's (left) side of the cockpit, activates the selected inverter through the

---

[17] The last maintenance work order for the airplane, dated January 23, 2001, did not list the total flying time.

[18] Hz is unit of frequency equal to one cycle per second.

inverter select relay and the avionics inverter select relay. If the selected inverter is inoperative, an inverter annunciator light will illuminate in the cockpit. The other inverter can then be selected, by moving the inverter select switch, to provide a.c. power to the airplane.

Avionics equipment powered by a.c. electricity includes the pilot-side altimeter (26 volts a.c.), the radio magnetic indicators (RMI, 115 volts a.c.), and the air data computer (115 volts a.c.). The air data computer produces electrical output signals for air data displays, the pilot-side attitude indicator, the autopilot, and mode C altitude information from the transponder.[19]

Postaccident examination and testing of a King Air 200 airplane that was similarly equipped to N81PF revealed that, if the airplane's a.c. electrical power were lost, flags would appear on most of the instruments on the pilot's (left) side of the cockpit, including the altimeter,[20] attitude indicator, horizontal situation indicator (HSI), radio altimeter, RMI, and altitude preselect. Also, a flag would appear on the RMI and HSI on the copilot's (right) side of the cockpit if the airplane's a.c. electrical power were lost.

Further, the examination and testing determined that, if a.c. power were lost, the working instruments on the pilot's side of the cockpit would be limited to an airspeed indicator and a turn and slip indicator. The copilot's side of the cockpit would display working airspeed and turn and slip indicators but would also display a working altimeter and attitude indicator. The two pilot-side instruments and the four copilot-side instruments would function because they would receive inputs from the pitot static or vacuum systems.

The airplane's electrical system also includes an a.c. volt/frequency meter. The meter displays the frequency of the airplane's a.c. power in Hz and shows the a.c. voltage when the "push for volts" button is depressed. The meter's crossarm assembly has three short arms and one long arm with a needle attached. The needle arm's normal reading indicates 400 Hz/115 volts. The needle arm would be in the 380-Hz/100-volt position (the lowest reading on the meter) if the airplane had no a.c. power.[21]

Figure 2 shows a schematic of the King Air 200 a.c. electrical system. The figure shows that the inverter select relay, the avionics inverter select relays, and the inverter select switch are located between the inverters and the volt/frequency meter.

---

[19] Mode A identifying information from the transponder is powered by d.c. electricity.

[20] According to the manufacturer of the airplane's air data computer, the altimeter flag would also appear if the air data computer became invalid.

[21] According to the Beechcraft Super King Air 200 Pilot's Operating Handbook, the inverter annunciator light appears when the volt/frequency meter is at the 380-Hz/100-volt position.

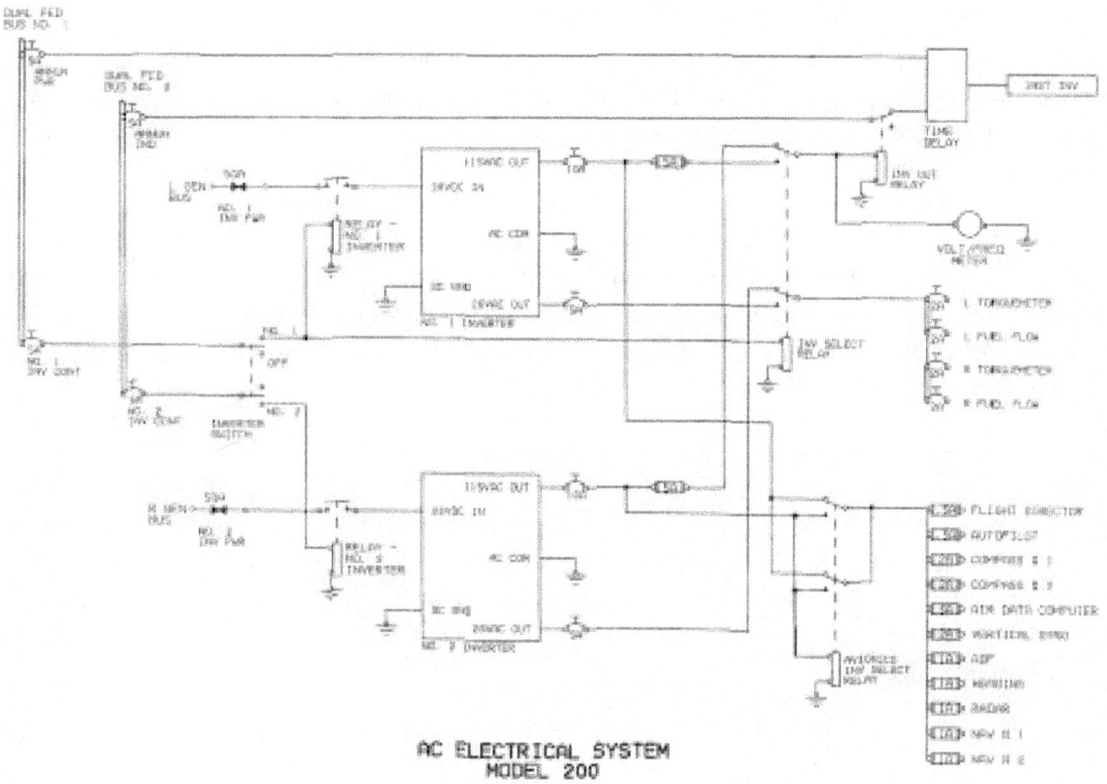

Source: Beechcraft Super King Air 200 Pilot's Operating Handbook.

Figure 2. Schematic of the King Air 200 a.c. electrical system.

1.6.1.1 Manufacturer Information

The Beechcraft Super King Air 200 Pilot's Operating Handbook, Section III, "Emergency Procedures," dated October 1978, indicates that the following actions should be taken for an electrical system failure:

CIRCUIT BREAKER TRIPPED [22]

1. Nonessential circuit – DO NOT RESET IN FLIGHT
2. Essential circuit:
    a. Circuit Breaker – PUSH TO RESET
    b. If Circuit Breaker trips again – DO NOT RESET

INVERTER INOPERATIVE

– Select the other inverter

---

[22] The circuit breaker panel assembly is located on the right side of the cockpit at knee level.

1.6.2 Maintenance Records

A review of the maintenance records for the accident airplane indicated that the airplane was maintained from 1976 to September 2000 using either an FAA- or a manufacturer-approved continuous inspection program. One of these programs was administered by the Pennsylvania Department of Transportation (PennDOT), which purchased the airplane in 1989. Specifically, in 1994, PennDOT's Bureau of Aviation submitted a request to the FAA for an Approved Aircraft Continuous Inspection Program for the King Air 200. The program consisted of one primary and three interim inspections conducted by an appropriately rated repair station or a qualified certificated mechanic. The time between primary inspections was not to exceed 600 hours, and each of the interim inspections was to be performed at 150-hour intervals.

The FAA approved PennDOT's request on June 22, 1994, and the inspection program was first used on N81PF on April 23, 1996, when a second interim inspection was performed. At the time of the inspection, the airplane had accumulated about 7,491 hours of total flying time. PennDOT designed its own discrepancy sheets to track the discrepancies found during inspections and to show the corrective action taken in response. These discrepancy sheets were required to be a part of the airplane's permanent maintenance records.

On August 18, 1999, PennDOT sold N81PF; at that time, the airplane had accumulated about 8,547 hours total flying time. On September 30, 1999, the airplane was sold to North Bay Charter, its owner at the time of the accident. North Bay Charter leased the airplane to Navajo Aviation of Concord, California, which operated the airplane under 14 CFR Part 135. Navajo Aviation had received permission from the FAA and PennDOT to continue using PennDOT's inspection program for the remaining two interim inspections in the four-inspection cycle. Navajo Aviation noted discrepancies on its own discrepancy sheets but did not include all of the sheets in the airplane's permanent maintenance records. (The Safety Board requested, and Navajo Aviation provided, copies of those discrepancy forms that were not included in the records.) According to the owner of North Bay Charter, the airplane was removed from Navajo Aviation's Part 135 operating certificate on September 16, 2000; after that date, the accident pilot managed the airplane from PWA.[23]

The most recent primary inspection of N81PF was performed by PennDOT on February 12, 1999, when the airplane had accumulated about 8,361 hours total flying time. The most recent first interim inspection was performed by PennDOT on July 23, 1999, when the airplane had accumulated about 8,510 hours total flying time. The most recent second interim inspection was performed by Navajo Aviation on June 28, 2000, when the airplane had accumulated about 8,659 hours total flying time. The airplane had not reached the interval for its next third interim inspection, so the most recent one was performed by PennDOT on August 14, 1998, when the airplane had accumulated about 8,213 hours total flying time.

---

[23] See sections 1.17.1 and 1.17.2 for more information.

A review of the maintenance records through June 28, 2000 (when the last second interim inspection was performed), revealed no uncorrected maintenance discrepancies. After September 16, 2000 (when the airplane was removed from Navajo's certificate), the airplane underwent various maintenance repairs at different maintenance facilities. According to the owner of the airplane, no major maintenance had been performed after the airplane had been moved back to PWA.

The maintenance records noted a discrepancy on October 23, 1990, involving both inverters. Specifically, the pilot at that time reported that both inverters were inoperative in flight and that a.c. power was restored after 5 to 8 minutes. The cause of the problem was found to be a failed relay rather than inoperative inverters. The failed relay was replaced, and no further discrepancies regarding the inverters were reported. The maintenance records also showed that the No. 1 inverter was replaced in May 1996 with an overhauled inverter and that the No. 2 inverter was replaced in October 1994 with a new inverter. The maintenance records did not indicate any discrepancies regarding either of these inverters.

A review of FAA Service Difficulty Reports for the King Air 200 electrical system found that 89 reports had been submitted between January 28, 1986, and December 1, 2000. Eight of these reports involved inverters, but none of the reports involved a dual inverter failure.

1.7 Meteorological Information

Air traffic control tower (ATCT) personnel certified by the NWS under the Supplemental Aviation Weather Reporting System make weather observations at BJC. The weather conditions reported at 1658 and 1745 were as follows: wind variable at 4 knots, visibility 1 mile in light snow, sky obscured with vertical visibility 200 feet, temperature -4° C, dew point -5° C, and altimeter setting 30.00 inches of Hg.

The closest airport to the accident site is Front Range Airport in Denver, located about 14 miles west of the site, but the airport's weather observations are only transmitted locally and are not archived. The closest official weather reporting facilities to the accident site are Denver International Airport, located about 20 miles west-northwest of the site; Centennial Airport in Denver, located about 24 miles west-southwest of the site; and Buckley Air Force Base in Aurora, located 23 miles west of the site.

Denver International Airport has an automated surface observing system (ASOS) that is maintained by the NWS and augmented by NWS certified weather observers.[24] At 1715, the ASOS indicated that visibility was 1 1/2 miles in light snow and mist and that the sky condition was ceiling overcast at 1,500 feet. At 1742, the ASOS indicated that

---

[24] The ASOS continuously measures wind, visibility, precipitation and obstructions to vision, cloud height, sky cover, dew point, and altimeter setting. The certified weather observers can provide observations for any other operationally significant information and override the automated mode if it malfunctions or provides unrepresentative values.

visibility was 1 1/2 miles in light snow and mist and that the sky condition was scattered clouds at 600 feet and ceiling overcast at 1,300 feet. Centennial Airport is equipped with an automated weather observing system (AWOS) that is augmented by NWS certified weather observers.[25] At 1653, the AWOS reported that the visibility was 1 mile in light snow and mist and that the sky condition was ceiling broken at 600 feet and overcast at 1,500 feet. At 1753, the AWOS reported that visibility was 1 mile in light snow and mist and that the sky condition was ceiling broken at 800 feet, second broken layer of clouds at 4,200 feet, and overcast at 6,000 feet. Weather observers at Buckley Air Force Base reported, at 1656 and 1755, that visibility was 1 mile in light snow and mist and that the sky condition was ceiling broken at 600 feet and overcast at 1,100 feet.[26]

The closest Weather Surveillance Radar 1988 Doppler (WSR-88D) is located at Front Range Airport. The WSR-88D is a 10-centimeter S-band wavelength radar that provides a three-dimensional volume scan of the atmosphere at varying degrees of elevation. Before and after the accident, the WSR-88D was displaying the five lowest elevation angles (0.4°, 1.5°, 2.5°, 3.5°, and 4.5°) every 10 minutes. The 4.5° elevation scan that covered the period from 1728:56 to 1738:37 indicated very light weather echoes under the accident airplane's flight track.

The WSR-88D also produces a vertical azimuth display wind profile. The wind profile is based on the detection of echoes within 20 miles of the radar site. The profile between 1709 and 1728 detected echoes to 28,000 feet. At 1738, the profile detected the wind at 22,000 feet from 180° at 35 knots, the wind at 24,000 feet from 180° at 40 knots, and droplets up to 26,000 feet.

Geostationary Operational Environmental Satellite number 10 (referred to as "GOES-10") infrared satellite imagery at 1730 depicted a large cloud shield over the accident area. The sounding data from these images indicated that the cloud tops were about 27,000 feet.

Three NWS AIRMETs were current during the time of the accident flight for eastern Colorado, including the area of the accident site.[27] All three were issued at 1345 and were valid until 2000. One of the AIRMETs warned of occasional moderate rime to mixed icing in clouds and in precipitation below 22,000 feet. Another AIRMET warned of occasional moderate turbulence below 18,000 feet associated with moderate southerly to

---

[25] The AWOS is another system that measures, collects, and disseminates weather information. According to the FAA's Web site, the basic difference between ASOS and AWOS is that ASOS generally comprises a standard suite of weather sensors that have all been procured from one contractor, whereas AWOS is a suite of weather sensors of many different configurations that were either procured by the FAA or purchased by individuals, groups, or airports that are required to meet FAA standards to be able to report weather parameters.

[26] All three of these weather reporting facilities reported similar information concerning the wind (generally from the northeast with windspeeds under 5 knots), temperature and dew point (about -4° C), and altimeter setting (near 29.99 inches of Hg).

[27] No other NWS in-flight weather advisory category—SIGMET [significant meteorological information], Convective SIGMET, Severe Weather Forecast Alert, and Center Weather Advisory—was current at the time of the accident.

southeasterly flow. The last AIRMET warned of occasional widespread ceilings below 1,000 feet and visibility below 3 miles in precipitation and mist.

The Safety Board contacted two aviation research meteorologists from the National Center for Atmospheric Research in Boulder regarding the potential icing environment about the time of the accident. These meteorologists (who are well-known experts and leaders in the field of icing research) use an icing diagnostic program, known as the Integrated Icing Diagnostic Algorithm, which incorporates multiple sources of weather information to determine the threat of airframe icing and supercooled large droplets. Analysis of the program's output[28] for 1700 on the day of the accident indicated a fairly low threat for potential icing and no threat for potential supercooled large droplets over eastern Colorado, including the area of the accident site.

In addition, no pilot reports indicated any in-flight icing over Colorado surrounding the time of the accident.

1.7.1 Meteorological Information for N250FX and N77LX

The Learjet 60 (N250FX) was kept overnight at Centennial Airport from January 26 to 27, 2001. The pilot indicated that the airplane was deiced before departing for BJC about 1718 on January 27th. The pilot stated that the airplane climbed to an altitude of 7,200 feet. The pilot also stated that he flew in IMC with the anti-ice on and that the airplane did not accumulate any ice on its unprotected areas. He further stated that visibility was 1 mile and that snowfall was "moderate" during the approach. The airplane landed at BJC about 1726. The pilot indicated that the runway and taxiway had a thin layer of snow. After he parked the airplane, the pilot noticed snow beginning to accumulate on the upper wing surfaces. The airplane was subsequently deiced.

The passengers boarded the airplane for the return trip to SWO, and the airplane departed from BJC at 1808. The pilot stated that he entered clouds at about 300 feet and that, during the climb to 9,000 feet, he encountered "continuous light to moderate chop." The pilot further indicated that he encountered "continuous moderate chop" from 17,000 to 26,000 feet and that the flight was smooth between 26,000 and 33,000 feet, with the cloud tops at 33,000 feet. In addition, the pilot stated that, from 14,000 to 22,000 feet, the windshield accumulated ice even with the full bleed air windshield heat on. The airplane landed at SWO at 1919.

The Cessna Citation 650 (N77LX) was kept in a hangar overnight at BJC from January 26 to 27, 2001. The pilot stated that the airplane was in a hangar when the passengers boarded it for the return trip to SWO and that the airplane was warm with no accumulation of snow on the wings. He also stated that, during the departure, visibility was 1/2 mile in light snow and that, during the climb, the airplane did not accumulate any ice buildup on the center post of the windshield and there was "very occasional light

---

[28] At the time of this analysis, the Integrated Icing Diagnostic Algorithm was an experimental product for research purposes only. The product is now used by the NWS in its operations and is available on the Internet.

chop." In addition, he indicated that the cloud tops were at 29,000 feet and that the cruising altitude was 37,000 feet.

1.7.2 Additional Pilot Witness Statements Regarding the Weather Conditions

A Piper Cheyenne 3A pilot indicated that he was traveling from Albuquerque, New Mexico, to BJC and had landed about 10 minutes before the accident airplane departed. During the arrival into BJC, the Cheyenne pilot indicated that the airplane encountered moderate snow but did not encounter any ice or turbulence. He stated that the clouds were at 200 feet with 1-mile visibility. He also stated that the conditions at BJC were "not that bad."

Two pilots operating King Air airplanes landed at Front Range Airport (the closest airport to the accident site) between 1650 and 1750 on the day of the accident. One pilot indicated that he flew from Steamboat Springs, Colorado, at a cruising altitude of 17,000 feet and did not encounter any turbulence or icing en route or on approach to the airport. He reported that the sky condition was ceiling overcast at 400 feet and that visibility was obscured at about 1 mile in snow and mist. The second pilot was traveling from Grand Junction to Front Range with a stop at Centennial Airport. He indicated that no icing occurred en route to Centennial but that frost began to form on the airplane's wings after landing. After the airplane was deiced, it departed for Front Range Airport. The pilot stated that the airplane experienced light to moderate turbulence from 17,000 feet to the surface but did not accumulate any icing. Further, the pilot stated that the sky condition was overcast at 400 feet and that visibility was about 1 mile in snow and mist.

1.8   Aids to Navigation

No navigational aid problems were reported.

1.9   Communications

No communications problems were reported between the pilot and any of the air traffic controllers that handled the flight.

1.10   Airport Information

1.10.1 Air Traffic Control Information

The Denver TRACON is located at Denver International Airport. Three controllers at the TRACON handled N81PF on the day of the accident.

The first controller, who handled N81PF at the Departure Radar Four position, had been a U.S. Air Force tower controller from 1976 to 1986. He began working for the FAA in December 1986, was assigned to the Denver ATCT in March 1987, and transferred to the Denver TRACON in October 1990. He became fully certified at the Denver TRACON in February 1995.

The second controller, who also handled N81PF at the Departure Radar Four position, began working for the FAA in July 1986 and was assigned to the Standiford, Kentucky, ATCT in November 1986. He transferred to the Covington, Kentucky, ATCT in March 1990 and the Denver TRACON in September 1998. He became fully certified at the Denver TRACON in June 1999.

The third controller, who handled N81PF at the Satellite Radar Two position, began working for the FAA in July 1982 at the ATCT and TRACON at Bradley International Airport, Windsor Locks, Connecticut. He transferred to the Denver TRACON in January 1992, returned to the Bradley TRACON in September 1996, and transferred back to the Denver TRACON in September 1998. The controller became fully certified at the Denver TRACON in December 1998.

The first Departure Radar Four controller indicated that, after departing from BJC, the airplane turned to the assigned heading, and its climb appeared "normal." After the controller cleared the airplane to proceed directly to the EPKEE intersection, the second Departure Radar Four controller arrived to take over the position. According to the first controller, during the position relief briefing, both controllers noticed that the airplane was not turning directly to the EPKEE intersection but was still flying on a 060° heading. The second controller indicated that he issued instructions for the airplane to fly on a 110° heading because he thought that the pilot had not followed the clearance to proceed directly to the EPKEE intersection. The first controller also indicated that the pilot appeared to have a slow response to the clearance to proceed directly to the EPKEE intersection.

The second Departure Radar Four controller reported that the airplane turned to the newly assigned heading in a timely manner and that everything appeared "normal." This controller also reported that he continued to watch the radar target until the airplane left his airspace and that he saw nothing unusual during this time.

The Satellite Radar Two controller indicated that, when he cleared the pilot to proceed directly to the EPKEE intersection, the airplane appeared to be tracking the course well. The controller also indicated that radar contact with the airplane was lost when the airplane was about 10 miles southwest of Byers, Colorado.[29] The controller stated that the airplane was at an altitude of 23,000 feet at the time. Further, he stated that, before the airplane's radar target disappeared, the airplane seemed to be "doing fine" and did not appear to have any problems with its mode C altitude information.

---

[29] Byers, Colorado, is located about 3 miles southeast of the accident site.

About 1738:05 and 1738:17, the Satellite Radar Two controller attempted to contact the airplane. About 1738:28, the controller contacted the Denver ARTCC East Departure Controller to see if he had radar contact with the airplane, and he indicated that radar contact with the airplane had been lost. The Satellite Radar Two controller tried continually to contact the airplane and looked at the Departure Four Right radar display (which uses a different radar site than the one used at the Satellite Radar Two position) to try to locate the airplane.

About 1739:40, the Satellite Radar Two controller asked the pilot of United Airlines flight 1270, who was on frequency, to attempt to contact the airplane; the pilot tried but reported that he received no response. About 1742:00, the TRACON was informed by the county sheriff's office that an airplane accident had occurred near Strasburg. About 1747:40, the controller asked the pilot of Northwest Airlines flight 800, who was on frequency, to determine if that airplane was receiving a signal from an emergency locator transmitter, but the pilot responded that no signal was being received.

1.11 Flight Recorders

The accident airplane was not equipped with a cockpit voice recorder or a flight data recorder. Title 14 CFR Part 91 did not require the airplane to be so equipped.

1.12 Wreckage and Impact Information

The accident airplane's wreckage was located about 42 miles east of BJC. All of the major pieces of the airplane's structure were recovered and examined. The wreckage was spread across snow-covered rolling terrain over a distance of 2,800 feet. The airplane's first impact point made a 20- by 30-foot impression in the ground. The wreckage path was oriented along a 135° magnetic heading. The main wreckage site was at a ground elevation of about 5,200 feet and was located about 1/2 nm southeast of the location of the last mode A transponder return.

All structural pieces found before the main wreckage area exhibited no evidence of fire damage. The first debris items found along the wreckage path were small, lightweight pieces from the right horizontal stabilizer rear spar enclosure panel, which were located about 2,700 feet northwest of the main wreckage. Several sections of the right horizontal stabilizer upper and lower skins were found next along the wreckage path. The first large piece of wreckage found was the left horizontal stabilizer, which was located about 1,500 feet northwest of the main wreckage. An 11-foot section of the right outboard wing was found about 1,100 feet northwest of the main wreckage.

The main wreckage, which consisted of the cockpit, forward fuselage, nose landing gear, left inboard wing and flap, and fuselage belly, was located 125 feet southeast of the first impact point. These structures came to rest in an inverted position and exhibited fire damage. The fuselage belly showed no impact damage, but the cockpit and fuselage crown area showed severe impact damage.

The left horizontal stabilizer main spar lower cap was bent aft and downward. The front spar upper and lower caps were fractured and bent downward. The right horizontal stabilizer fractured into numerous small pieces, and the upper and lower skins exhibited saw-tooth tear features and screw curls at various locations. No evidence of preexisting corrosion or fatigue cracks was found.

The right wing fractured outboard of the engine. The upper skin surface was displaced downward over the ribs and stringers, and the sheet metal frame and skin at the fracture location were bent downward. The main spar upper cap was fractured and bent up 60°. The main spar lower cap was bent upward at the fracture location, and the fracture surface exhibited no evidence of fatigue or corrosion. The rear spar upper cap had fractured at the inboard aileron hinge, and the upper skin between the fracture location and the inboard aileron hinge was bent downward. The rear spar lower cap was fractured outboard of the inboard edge of the aileron and was bent upward 30°. No evidence of preexisting corrosion or fatigue cracks was found. The left wing also fractured outboard of the engine. The upper and lower caps of the main and rear spars remained attached to the left wing outboard section, but deformation on these caps could not be determined because of fire damage.

The two engines, two propeller hubs, and six propeller blades were all recovered from the crash site. The engines showed no indication of an in-flight fire, uncontainment, case rupture, or preimpact failure. The engines' rotors had blade and vane breakage and bending that were consistent with rotation at the time of impact. The propeller hubs had separated from the engines, and one propeller blade had separated from each hub. On April 18, 2001, the propellers were examined at the manufacturer's facility in Piqua, Ohio. The examination revealed witness marks on the propeller pistons' rear spring retainer cans and the blades' butts that were consistent with the blades being in the normal operating range at the time of impact.

The pilot-side altimeter was crushed, but the faceplate was legible. No needle was present, and the flag position could not initially be determined. Removal of the faceplate revealed that the altitude reading was 23,220 feet and that the flag was in the visible position. The copilot-side altimeter was not recovered. The pilot-side attitude indicator was damaged by impact forces and fire. Disassembly of the unit showed witness marks that were consistent with a wings-level and an approximately 10° nose-down position. The copilot-side attitude indicator was not recovered. Both RMIs were damaged by impact forces and fire, all face glass was missing, and flag positions could not be determined. One RMI still had its needles, but they were bent; the other RMI was missing its needles. Both RMI compass cards showed a heading of 115°. Both HSIs were damaged by impact forces and fire, the faceplate on each was illegible, and the needles were missing. The air data computer case was fractured, and most of the internal components were missing. The radio altimeter casing had partially folded over the faceplate, and the needle was missing.

Only one airspeed indicator and one turn and slip indicator were recovered. Their data plates were damaged, so no determination could be made as to whether the indicators were on the pilot's or copilot's side of the cockpit. The mounting plate on the airspeed indicator was intact, but most of the face glass and the needle were missing. The case for the turn and slip indicator was fractured, all of the face glass was missing, and no needle was present.

The a.c. volt/frequency meter was discovered at the accident site almost 3 months after the accident, after snow had melted. The meter was found loose on the ground, and its faceplate mechanism had separated from the unit case. The needle arm was displaced to the right. The meter face showed two witness marks aligned with the 380-Hz/100-volt position.

The No. 1 and No. 2 inverters were found broken, and their internal components and wiring were destroyed. The internal fuses for both inverters were broken but not melted or burned. The inverter select switch, inverter select relay, and avionics inverter select relay were not recovered from the wreckage. The circuit breaker panel had broken away from the airplane and showed impact and postcrash fire damage. Almost all of the circuit breakers were found in the open position.

One emergency oxygen mask and hose assembly was recovered. The bag included in the assembly showed several cuts, rips, and holes in a repeating pattern. The bag was not inflated, and the hose was still attached to the assembly.

1.13 Medical and Pathological Information

Tissue specimens from the pilot and second pilot were sent to the FAA's Civil Aerospace Medical Institute in Oklahoma City, Oklahoma, for toxicological analysis. The specimens tested negative for major drugs of abuse and for prescription and over-the-counter medications. The pilot's specimens tested positive for ethanol, but the analysis indicated that the detected ethanol might have been the result of postmortem ethanol formation rather than ethanol ingestion. The second pilot's specimens also tested positive for ethanol, but the analysis indicated that the detected ethanol was the result of postmortem ethanol formation.

1.14 Fire

A fuel-fed fire erupted after the airplane impacted the ground.

1.15 Survival Aspects

Autopsy results indicated that the cause of death for all of the airplane occupants was multiple massive blunt traumatic injuries.

1.16 Tests and Research

1.16.1 Airplane Performance Study

The Safety Board conducted an airplane performance study to develop the time history of the airplane's motion and to calculate various performance parameters. To perform the study, several sources of information were used, including the ATC transcript, ASR radar data from the Denver TRACON, National Track Analysis Program radar data from the Denver ARTCC, aerodynamic data from the airplane's manufacturer, and weather data.

Radar data showed that, after its departure from BJC, the airplane executed a right turn to the northeast while climbing through 7,600 feet. The airplane continued its climb to the northeast until about 1724:07, when the airplane was at an altitude of 13,500 feet and the departure controller directed the pilot to turn to the right on a southeast heading. About 1732:50, the airplane was at an altitude of 23,100 feet and was maintaining its heading to the southeast.

Because mode C transponder information was not transmitted after about 1735:44, the airplane's altitude time history had to be estimated after this time. As a result, calculations of the airplane's performance parameters are approximations.

Several seconds after the last mode C transponder return, the airplane banked slightly in the right-wing-down direction. Calculated performance parameters showed that, by 1736:15, the airplane's airspeed was about 200 knots, its bank was 30° right wing down, and its pitch was 15° airplane nose down. Radar data indicated that, by 1736:26, the airplane started to deviate from its heading and make a right turn to the south. During the next 30 seconds, the airplane's bank angle continued to increase in the right-wing-down direction, and its pitch angle remained near 20° airplane nose down.

About 1736:45, the airplane had turned to the north and was continuing its turn to the right. At that point, the airplane's altitude was about 17,200 feet, and its airspeed had accelerated to about 250 knots. The airplane's right bank, nose-down pitch, and airspeed continued to increase as the airplane completed a 360° rotation in heading by 1737:02. During the time that the airplane was executing the 360° turn, its descent rate was increasing constantly to more than 15,000 feet per minute. By 1737:10, the airplane entered a steep dive; at that point, the airplane was descending through 10,000 feet with its pitch angle exceeding 80° airplane nose down and its bank angle exceeding 100° right wing down.

Calculated performance parameters showed that, about the time of the last mode A transponder return (1737:12), the airplane rolled to the left toward wings level, its descent rate began to be arrested, and its nose-down pitch decreased. During the next 5 seconds, the airplane's airspeed increased rapidly to more than 350 knots as the descent rate was reduced. The calculated performance parameters also showed that, by 1737:15, the airplane was on a 130° heading at an altitude of 6,200 feet.

1.17 Organizational and Management Information

1.17.1 Jet Express Services

The pilot was the sole proprietor of Jet Express Services, an aircraft management company located at PWA. The pilot managed two airplanes, including the accident airplane. He arranged lease agreements for the two airplanes and charged fees for his management services. Among Jet Express Services' clients and users of the accident airplane were the Oklahoma Department of Public Safety and the Oklahoma Gas and Electric Company.

According to OSU's Vice President of Business and External Relations, the accident pilot flew for the university's Athletic Department. OSU records indicated that, between July 1, 2000, and January 25, 2001 (the day before the flight from SWO to BJC), the pilot flew three roundtrips for OSU athletic events. On October 14, 2000, the pilot flew to Birmingham, Alabama, for a men's golf event, returning 2 days later. On November 26, 2000, the pilot flew to Denton, Texas, for a men's basketball event, returning the next day. On January 16, 2001, the pilot flew to Waco, Texas, for a men's basketball event, returning the next day.

1.17.2 North Bay Charter

North Bay Charter, LLC, was chartered in Nevada. The owner of the company was also the owner of the accident airplane. As stated in section 1.6.2, the owner leased the airplane to Navajo Aviation of California. According to the owner of North Bay Charter, business for the airplane was slow, so he placed the airplane in Oklahoma with the accident pilot for 3 months. (During this time, the airplane continued to operate under Navajo's Part 135 certificate.) Afterward, the airplane was returned to California. The General Manager of Navajo Aviation indicated that the airplane was not being chartered for many flights and that, according to his records, its last company charter flight occurred on August 10, 2000. The General Manager also indicated that, when the owner terminated his relationship with Navajo Aviation, the airplane was immediately removed from Navajo's Part 135 certificate. The airplane was sent back to Oklahoma and was again managed by the accident pilot. The owner dry leased[30] the airplane per hour and paid the pilot a flat monthly fee to oversee the airplane. The owner also paid monthly hangar fees and maintenance bills for the airplane.

The owner of the accident airplane indicated that the airplane had been used for OSU travel a few times since he had acquired the airplane.

---

[30] AC 91-37A, "Truth in Leasing," states that a dry lease is the "leasing of an aircraft without the crew."

1.17.3 Federal Aviation Administration Surveillance

On March 24, 1998, an FAA air safety inspector administered a Part 135 check ride to the pilot in a King Air 200. The purpose of the check ride was to add the pilot to the Part 135 certificate held by Million Air in Oklahoma City. (The air safety inspector was also the principal operations inspector for Million Air.) The inspector indicated that one part of the check ride involved a simulated engine failure as the airplane climbed through 400 feet altitude with the autopilot engaged. According to FAA records, the airplane drifted off its heading by 30° and lost 100 feet of altitude before the air safety inspector intervened and told the pilot to manually fly the airplane. The air safety inspector said that the pilot thought that the autopilot would fly the airplane with the engine failure. The pilot failed the check ride. He received training and satisfactorily completed the check ride on the next day.

In a postaccident interview, the air safety inspector[31] indicated that the pilot "had a tendency to lock in on a problem and not fly the airplane." Also, the inspector stated that the pilot and N81PF were subsequently removed from the Million Air Part 135 certificate because the pilot had apparently flown the airplane for OSU without Million Air's knowledge.

On September 11, 1997, the pilot was providing proficiency training in a King Air 200 to FAA safety inspectors from the Airman Testing Standards Branch and was involved in a landing in which the nose gear actuator failed and was unable to lock down. The pilot landed the airplane on its two main landing gear wheels and on its nose. No one aboard the airplane was injured, and the airplane received only minor damage to its propellers. The FAA sent the pilot a letter of commendation, dated September 22, 1997, complimenting him for the manner in which he handled the emergency.

1.17.4 Federal Aviation Administration Letter to the Safety Board

In a January 25, 2002, letter to the Safety Board, the FAA recognized that North Bay Charter owned the accident airplane. However, the FAA stated that, for the accident flight, the airplane was being operated by Jet Express Services, which also provided the PIC. The FAA indicated that the pilot was required to operate the accident airplane pursuant to 14 CFR Part 135 because he had the primary responsibility for providing the airplane and the pilot services and was receiving compensation for both. The FAA added that the compensation was "direct and indirect."

---

[31] The air safety inspector is now the Director of Operations for Sierra Aviation doing business as Million Air Oklahoma City Aircraft Charter.

The FAA also stated the following:

> In Part 91 operations, the owner or operator bears the responsibility for the operation of the aircraft. The owner may exercise his responsibility by individually operating the aircraft or through the use of a flight department, through use of the services of a management company, or by hiring pilots. In Part 135 operations, the air carrier or commercial operator has the responsibility for operational control. In either case, of course, the pilot-in-command is primarily responsible for the safe operation of the flight.

Further, the FAA indicated that it determined that the Learjet and the Cessna Citation were fractionally owned and were being operated pursuant to 14 CFR Part 91. The FAA noted that a portion of the cost of these flights was also donated. The FAA stated that, "the fact that the cost of a given flight may be donated, whether in whole or in part, does not itself determine whether the flight is one required to be operated pursuant to Part 91 or Part 135. That determination depends upon an examination of the specific facts of each situation."

1.18 Additional Information

1.18.1 Oklahoma State University Travel Information

OSU's air transportation team travel policy in effect at the time of the accident was detailed in OSU policy and procedures document 3-0155, "Transportation Services Flight Department," dated April 2000. The document indicated that the university's Transportation Services Flight Department was to provide transportation for university and state employees, student athletes, and others traveling on official university or state business. The Flight Department Manager was responsible for administering OSU's air transportation policies at that time.

The policy and procedures document indicated that the Flight Department operated a six-seat Cessna 421B[32] and had access to other multiengine aircraft through the University of Oklahoma and the State of Oklahoma.[33] These airplanes could be operated during day or night and in VFR or IFR conditions. According to the Manager of the Flight Department, who is also the OSU Chief Pilot, all of the airplanes operated under 14 CFR Part 91. The document indicated that these airplanes were to be flown only by pilots from the OSU Flight Department or qualified pilots hired by the Flight Department Manager. The pilots were required to have a commercial pilot's license; certification for single-engine, multiengine, and instrument flying; and 2,500 hours as PIC, at least 500 of which were to have been in a multiengine airplane.

---

[32] OSU's Vice President of Business and External Relations stated that the Cessna 421B was too small to be used for athletic events.

[33] The Manager of the Flight Department indicated that the University of Oklahoma operated a Turbo Commander 690 and that the State of Oklahoma operated a King Air 350.

According to the policy and procedures document, the basic requirement for arranging transportation services was approval by the Flight Department Manager. The document also indicated that, for out-of-state transportation, prior approval from the appropriate OSU vice president was necessary. In addition, the document indicated that the judgment of a pilot would always prevail regarding whether flight conditions were safe for takeoff or continuation of a flight. Further, if the weather or the length of a trip were such that the pilot felt a copilot was necessary for the safe completion of the flight, the pilot would have the authority to dispatch a copilot for that purpose.

The policy and procedures document also stated that flights to be chartered for the university had to be contracted through the Flight Department. (Football team and commercial airline travel were exempt from this requirement.) The document explained that charter trips included any trips for which money, goods, or services were exchanged for air service. The Flight Department Manager was responsible for ensuring that all charter companies providing services to OSU were properly certified under FAA regulations (14 CFR Part 135). The proper certification was to be updated annually and kept on file within the department.

OSU indicated that, from July 1, 1999, to January 31, 2001, 62 charter flights had been arranged through the Flight Department, 50 of which were for athletic events. (An additional four charter flights were used for football team travel, but these flights were not contracted through the Flight Department.) According to the OSU Flight Department Manager, four Part 135 operators were on file with the Flight Department at the time of the accident, none of which were Jet Express Services.

According to OSU's Vice President of Business and External Relations, several alumni donate airplanes for the Athletic Department to use to transport players to games and events. The OSU policy and procedures document indicated that all airplanes donated for OSU use had to be certified and approved through the Flight Department. Information regarding the airplane's inspection records and insurance policy, the pilot's FAA certificate number and medical certificate, and the pilot's biennial flight review record were to be updated annually and kept on file within the department. OSU indicated that its Flight Department did not have any records on file regarding the accident pilot, second pilot, or airplane.

Donated flights did not require coordination with the Flight Department, and the only charges that the university incurred for such flights were for the pilots' hotel rooms, meals, and telephone use. According to the OSU Flight Department Manager, most donated flights were aboard personal airplanes being operated under 14 CFR Part 91. OSU indicated that 18 flights had been donated during the 2000 to 2001 basketball season.

OSU's Vice President of Business and External Relations stated that the flights that were used to transport OSU basketball players and associated personnel between SWO and BJC on January 26 and 27, 2001, were donated. The basketball staff coordinated these flights directly with the donors. The chairman of an Oklahoma City oil company, who was an OSU alumnus and a friend of the pilot, donated the use of N81PF.[34] In a postaccident interview, another friend of the pilot said that the donor paid for the airplane's rental fee, fuel, and associated expenses. This friend also said that the pilot did not bill OSU for his services because he enjoyed being with the basketball team players and coach and that he mostly flew for OSU as a single pilot because the athletic department staff wanted to use all of the available seats in the airplane.

1.18.1.1 Revised Team Travel Policy

On April 22, 2002, OSU issued a revised team travel policy "to provide a framework for safe and efficient athletic team travel"[35] and "to assign responsibility and accountability for enforcement." The policy states that the OSU Director of Intercollegiate Athletics is responsible for the overall administration of the revised policy and that a member of the athletic department staff is responsible for compliance, oversight, and recordkeeping. The director or a designee is to provide a copy of the policy to every coach, provide training to every coach, and maintain a signed statement from each coach indicating that he/she has read and understands the policy.

According to the policy, the OSU Director of Intercollegiate Athletics or a designee is also responsible for verifying that the mode of transportation recommended for use for athletic travel complies with the policy. Coaches are responsible for developing their season travel plans, including recommended transportation mode, and gaining written approval from the appropriate associate athletic director in advance of the season or subsequent schedule change. In addition, the policy indicates that any coach or athletic department staff member who knowingly violates the policy will be suspended until the director or a designee investigates the violation and that violations may result in disciplinary action or termination.

Section 6.01, "Types of Vehicles Used for Team Travel and Requirements for Operation," Subheading E, "Air Transportation," states that commercial air carriers, charter, time-share, and other aircraft may be used for athletic team travel. Section 6.01, subheadings A through D, address automobiles/minivans, 12- and 15-passenger vans,[36] buses, and mini-buses (20 to 30 passengers), respectively. OSU's revised team travel policy appears in appendix B.

1.18.2 Spatial Disorientation Information

Spatial disorientation occurs when a pilot has inadequate visual information or fails to attend to or properly interpret available information regarding the airplane's pitch

---

[34] An OSU alumnus from Houston, Texas, donated the use of the Learjet. A friend of the coach from Little Rock, Arkansas, donated the use of the Cessna Citation.

[35] The policy applies to baseball, basketball (women's and men's), equestrian, football, golf (women's and men's), soccer, softball, tennis (women's and men's), track (women's and men's indoor, outdoor, and cross country), and wrestling teams, as well as mascots, spirit squad members, student trainers, and student managers.

[36] OSU's revised team travel policy states that 12-passenger vans are to carry no more than 8 passengers and equipment and that 15-passenger vans are to carry no more than 10 passengers and equipment.

and bank. Instead, a disoriented pilot relies on cues that are often misleading. The most hazardous illusions that lead to spatial disorientation result from ambiguous information received from motion sensing organs located in each inner ear. The sensory organs of the inner ear detect angular accelerations in the pitch, yaw, and roll axes and gravity and linear accelerations. During flight, the inner ear organs may be stimulated by motion of the aircraft alone or along with head and body movement.

Spatial disorientation can occur in a banked airplane when it rolls very slowly at a rate that is not detected by the motion sensing organs of the inner ear. The threshold for the detection of roll rate (roll to bank) by humans is about 2° per second.[37] Spatial disorientation can also occur in a banked airplane when a constant-rate turn is maintained and stimulation of the inner ear organs ceases. A disoriented pilot who falsely perceives a constant-rate turn as a descent may respond with elevator pitch-up controls, which will tighten the turn. As the turn tightens and the airplane's bank continues to increase, the airplane will lose altitude from the resulting loss of vertical lift. A disoriented pilot who still perceives a wings-level flight attitude may respond to the loss of altitude with increased pitch-up controls, resulting in a steep spiral dive (commonly referred to as a "graveyard spiral").[38]

According to the FAA *Aeronautical Information Manual*, paragraph 8-1-5, spatial disorientation can only be prevented by visual reference to reliable fixed points on the ground or to flight instruments. FAA AC 60-4A, "Pilot's Spatial Disorientation," states that tests conducted with qualified instrument pilots showed that it could take as long as 35 seconds to establish full control solely by reference to flight instruments when a loss of visual reference occurs.

---

[37] A.J. Benson, "Spatial Disorientation—Common Illusions," eds. J. Ernsting, A.N. Nichols, and D.J. Rainford, *Aviation Medicine*, 3rd Ed. (Oxford, United Kingdom: Butterworth-Heinemann, 1999).

[38] The FAA *Aeronautical Information Manual*, Paragraph 8-1-5, "Illusions in Flight," describes a graveyard spiral as follows: "An observed loss of altitude during a coordinated constant-rate turn that has ceased stimulating the motion sensing system can create the illusion of being in a descent with the wings level. The disoriented pilot will pull back on the controls, tightening the spiral and increasing the loss of altitude."

2. Analysis

2.1 General

The pilot was properly certificated and qualified under Federal regulations. No evidence indicates any preexisting medical or behavioral conditions that might have adversely affected the pilot's performance during the accident flight.

The pilot filed an instrument flight rules (IFR) flight plan under 14 *Code of Federal* Regulations (CFR) Part 91 for the accident flight; as a result, he was the only person responsible for the airplane. In its January 25, 2002, letter to the Safety Board, the FAA determined that the pilot should have been operating the airplane under 14 CFR Part 135 because he had the primary responsibility for providing the airplane and the pilot services and was receiving compensation for both. The Board defers to the Federal Aviation Administration's (FAA) judgment that the flight should have been operated under 14 CFR Part 135.

The second pilot was properly certificated and qualified under Federal regulations. The second pilot was not a required flight crewmember because the airplane was certified for single-pilot operation under 14 CFR Part 91. Even if the flight had been operated under 14 CFR Part 135, the second pilot would still not have been a required crewmember; the airplane was certified for single-pilot operation under Part 135 in IFR conditions because a three-axis autopilot was installed and operating.[39] (The use of the autopilot is discussed later in this analysis.) Because the flight was conducted with two qualified pilots and an operational autopilot and thus exceeded Part 135 requirements, the circumstances of this accident would not have been any different if the pilot had operated the flight under Part 135 rather than Part 91.

The accident airplane was properly certified, equipped, and maintained in accordance with Federal regulations. The recovered components showed no evidence of any preexisting structural, engine, or system failures. (The in-flight electrical system failure is addressed later.)

Snow was falling at Jefferson County Airport (BJC) in Colorado when the accident airplane departed for Stillwater Regional Airport (SWO) in Oklahoma, and instrument meteorological conditions (IMC) prevailed from the surface to altitudes above those of the accident airplane. However, icing was not a factor in this accident. No pilot reports surrounding the time of the accident indicated any in-flight icing over Colorado, and none of the pilot witnesses indicated any in-flight icing along or near the accident airplane's route of flight. Also, radar data for the accident airplane indicated no degradation of airplane performance (airspeed or altitude) consistent with ice accretion.

---

[39] This certification information is found in the Beechcraft Super King Air 200 Pilot's Operating Handbook, Section II, "Limitations," dated February 1979.

No evidence of a cabin pressurization problem was found. Also, the repeating cuts, rips, and holes on the bag included in the recovered oxygen mask and hose assembly were consistent with a bag that remained folded and unused.

This accident was not survivable for any of the airplane occupants because they were subjected to impact forces that exceeded the limits of human tolerance.

This analysis discusses the accident sequence, including the role of spatial disorientation. The analysis also describes the airplane breakup sequence and provides possible explanations for the loss of mode C altitude transponder information aboard the airplane. In addition, the analysis compares Oklahoma State University's (OSU) revised team travel policy with the one that was in place at the time of the accident.

2.2 Accident Sequence

Radar data indicated that the flight from BJC to SWO was routine until the airplane was at an altitude of 23,200 feet. At that point, the airplane stopped transmitting mode C altitude transponder information, which is generated from electrical output signals from the airplane's a.c.-powered air data computer. The airplane continued to transmit mode A identifying transponder information, which is generated from d.c. electrical power, until the time of impact. Thus, a total power loss aboard the airplane did not occur, but a partial or complete loss of a.c. power had occurred.

It was possible that the a.c. electrical malfunction involved a failure of the air data computer only. However, the pilot-side altimeter indicated that the altitude reading was 23,220 feet, which was consistent with the last reported altitude (23,200 feet) before the airplane stopped transmitting mode C information. Also, both radio magnetic indicator (RMI) compass cards showed a heading of 115°, which was consistent with the airplane's heading when mode C information was lost. (The pilot was flying the airplane on a 110° heading and indicated that he was going to be making a turn of about 3°.) In addition, witness marks on the volt/frequency meter showed that it was at the 380-Hertz/100-volt position (the lowest reading) at the time of impact,[40] indicating that no a.c. power was available. The Safety Board concludes that the physical evidence recovered from the wreckage site and the recorded radar data indicate that a complete loss of a.c. electrical power occurred aboard the airplane. Further, a.c. power was not restored any time after it was lost; if a.c. power had been restored, the altimeter would have shown an altitude lower than 23,220 feet.

The complete loss of a.c. electrical power would have rendered most of the pilot's flight instruments inoperative. The only instruments that would have been available to the pilot were those that were operated by the pitot static or vacuum systems. Specifically, on

---

[40] The position of the three short arms of the meter's crossarm assembly supported this reading, but the one long arm—the needle arm—was displaced clockwise. The witness marks were likely made by the needle arm during the initial impact; the needle arm was then likely displaced during the subsequent impact, resulting in a false position.

the left side of the cockpit, the airspeed indicator and the turn and slip indicator would have been operational; on the right side of the cockpit, the airspeed indicator, turn and slip indicator, altimeter, and attitude indicator would have been operational. Despite the loss of the airplane's primary flight instruments, the pilot made no radio transmissions to the controller after mode C information was lost.[41] (Between 1 minute 33 seconds and 1 minute 36 seconds elapsed between the time of the last mode C return and airplane impact.)

The airplane's air data computer also produces electrical output signals for the autopilot. Thus, the complete loss of a.c. power would have caused the autopilot to cease operating if it were being used. The Safety Board was unable to determine from the available evidence whether the pilot was flying the airplane with the autopilot engaged or whether he was manually flying the airplane.

Ambient cockpit and instrument panel lighting are powered by d.c. electrical power. Thus, the pilot would have been able to see within the cockpit to attempt to diagnose the electrical problem. The flashing red master warning light and the autopilot disconnect annunciator light would have signaled the loss of the autopilot if it were engaged. Also, as demonstrated by postaccident examination and testing of a King Air 200 airplane that was similarly equipped to N81PF, instrument flags would have appeared on the pilot's altimeter, attitude indicator, horizontal situation indicator (HSI), radio altimeter, RMI, and altitude preselect. Examination of the pilot's altimeter verified that the instrument flag would have been visible to him.[42] In addition, the inverter annunciator light would have illuminated. The Safety Board concludes that the pilot would have had salient cues to identify the a.c. electrical power failure.

The pilot's experience and recent training should have prepared him to complete all prescribed checklist actions for diagnosing and resolving an electrical system failure. Further, it is possible that the second pilot would have been able to provide some assistance to the pilot. The postaccident examination and testing of a King Air 200 airplane showed that instrument flags would have appeared on the HSI and RMI on the second pilot's (right) side of the cockpit.[43] However, because the second pilot had not received any formal King Air training, he would have had limited experience with the airplane's systems and emergency procedures.

The Beechcraft Super King Air 200 Pilot's Operating Handbook indicates that, if one inverter is inoperative, the other should be selected using the inverter select switch.

---

[41] The communications radios were powered by the No. 1 and No. 2 d.c. avionics buses and were thus operational.

[42] The Safety Board could not determine whether the flags on the attitude indicator, HSI, radio altimeter, and RMI would have been visible to the pilot because the attitude indicator faceplate was illegible and the needles on the other instruments were missing. The altitude preselect flag appeared in the retracted position, indicating that it would not have been visible to the pilot. The flag would not be visible to the pilot if the autopilot was not in use, but, if the autopilot were in use, impact forces might have forced the flag into the retracted position.

[43] The Safety Board could not determine whether the flags on the HSI and RMI would have been visible to the second pilot because the needles on both instruments were missing.

This switch is located away from other switches on a panel below the instrument panel and to the left of the pilot-side control wheel. However, the Safety Board was unable to determine from the available evidence whether the pilot attempted to restore a.c. power using the inverter select switch.

The Beechcraft Super King Air 200 Pilot's Operating Handbook also indicates that, in the event of an electrical system failure, nonessential circuit breakers are not to be reset in flight, but essential circuit breakers are to be reset.[44] However, there was insufficient evidence to determine whether either pilot attempted to troubleshoot the electrical problem by examining the circuit breaker panel, which was located on the right side of the cockpit at knee level.

Despite the loss of a.c. electrical power, the pilot could have safely flown and landed the airplane from the left seat by referencing the available (non-a.c.-powered) flight instruments on the right side of the cockpit (the altimeter and the airspeed, attitude, and turn and slip indicators). Also, the pilot could have asked the second pilot to fly the airplane because the available flight instruments would be more easily viewed from the right seat. The Safety Board could not determine from the available evidence what actions the pilot took (or did not take) and the extent to which the pilot might have coordinated with the second pilot. Nevertheless, the Safety Board concludes that the pilot did not appropriately manage the workload associated with troubleshooting the loss of a.c. electrical power with the need to establish and maintain positive control of the airplane.[45]

Because mode C data were unavailable after about 1735:44, the Safety Board's airplane performance study for this accident was used to estimate the airplane's altitude and descent rate after this point. According to air traffic control (ATC) radar data, the airplane began to turn to the right about 1736:26. The calculated bank angle during this turn, estimated to be less than 15° initially, increased to more than 80° over the next 30 seconds. Also, airplane performance calculations showed that the airplane entered into a descent shortly after starting the turn to the right. The estimated descent rate increased constantly to more than 15,000 feet per minute as the airplane completed a 360° turn. The Safety Board concludes that the airplane's estimated flightpath in the final 2 minutes of flight was consistent with a graveyard spiral resulting from pilot spatial disorientation.[46]

The pilot probably did not sense the right descending turn at first because the airplane's bank was entered gradually. As the airplane's bank angle and descent rate began increasing, the pilot's spatial disorientation most likely persisted, and he was not able to successfully use the available instruments to regain positive control of the airplane. Any head movements that the pilot made while attempting to diagnose the electrical system malfunction (for example, looking down and to the right at the circuit breaker panel)[47] might have exacerbated his spatial disorientation because the motion sensing organs of the

---

[44] Because all of the circuit breakers were found open, most likely because of impact forces, the Safety Board could not determine the positions of the circuit breakers at the time of the accident.

[45] In a postaccident interview, the air safety inspector who conducted the pilot's March 1998 Part 135 check ride indicated that the pilot tended to "lock in on a problem and not fly the airplane." This observation is consistent with the circumstances of this accident.

inner ear could have been stimulated by these head movements in addition to the motion of the airplane.

Radar data, ground scars, and wreckage distribution indicated that the airplane impacted terrain at an angle that was less steep than the descent. The Safety Board concludes that the airplane's angle at the time of impact indicated that the pilot attempted to arrest the descent in the final portion of the flight, possibly in response to obtaining visual references of the ground after emerging from the lowest layer of clouds.[48] The pilot input and the airplane reaction required to arrest the descent rate with the available altitude would have placed a large aerodynamic loading on the airplane. The aerodynamic loading caused the airplane to break apart in flight at a low altitude (within several hundred feet of the ground) and crash into terrain. The ATC primary radar data returns about 1737:16, 1737:21, and 1737:26 (see figure 1) and the scattered debris found at the accident site were also consistent with an in-flight breakup at a low altitude.

The cockpit and fuselage crown area showed severe impact damage, but the fuselage belly was not damaged. The airplane was found in an inverted position 125 feet from its initial impact point with the ground. Thus, the airplane initially impacted the ground nose first and then bounced 125 feet to an inverted position.

2.3 Breakup Sequence

On the basis of the wreckage distribution,[49] the Safety Board determined that the tail structure sections departed the airplane first and that the outboard section of the right wing departed the airplane after the tail sections. The pilot likely initiated a severe pull-up maneuver by pulling back on the control column; this action loaded the tail in the downward direction and the wing in the upward direction. The Safety Board concludes that the in-flight breakup occurred because the aerodynamic loading during the pilot's

---

[46] The Safety Board is not making any recommendations in this report regarding spatial disorientation because the FAA has already published many resources to acquaint pilots with the hazards of spatial disorientation. These resources include Advisory Circular (AC) 60-4A, "Pilot's Spatial Disorientation"; *Aeronautical Information Manual* Paragraph 8-1-5, "Illusions in Flight"; *Airplane Flying Handbook* (FAA-H-8083-3) Chapter 9, "Flight by Reference to Instruments"; *Instrument Flying Handbook* (FAA-H-8083-15) Chapter 1, "Human Factors"; AC 00-6A, "Aviation Weather"; AC 61-23C, "Pilot's Handbook of Aeronautical Knowledge"; and *Medical Facts for Pilots* (FAA-P-8740-41). In addition, the FAA has recently attempted to discover why the malfunctioning of attitude instruments in general aviation airplanes can result in loss of control in partial panel situations. See, for example, D.B. Beringer and J.D. Ball, "When gauges fail and clouds are tall, we miss the horizon most of all: General Aviation pilot responses to the loss of attitude information in IMC," *Proceedings of the 45th Annual Meeting of the Human Factors and Ergonomics Society* (Santa Monica, CA: Human Factors and Ergonomics Society, 2001), Vol. 45, 21-25.

[47] Research has demonstrated that visual distraction and head movements can often lead to spatial disorientation. See Benson, "Spatial Disorientation—Common Illusions," 1999.

[48] The closest official weather reporting facilities to the accident site—Denver International Airport, Centennial Airport, and Buckley Air Force Base—all reported that the lowest layer of clouds about the time of the accident was 600 feet.

[49] See section 1.12 for more information.

pull-up maneuver was great enough to overload the horizontal stabilizer downward and the right outboard wing section was sufficiently loaded upward to sustain a permanent bend in the spar. As soon as the horizontal stabilizer fractured and departed the airplane, the right outboard wing loaded downward and separated from the airplane in a downward direction.

2.4 Loss of A.C. Electrical Power

Four possibilities exist to explain the loss of a.c. power aboard the accident airplane. First, the selected inverter could have failed, and the pilot might not have switched to the other inverter. However, the pilot should have been familiar with this switch because it is always used to supply a.c. power after engine start and to terminate a.c. power before engine shutdown.

Second, a dual inverter failure could have occurred. However, it is extremely unlikely that both inverters would have failed because of the inverters' history of reliability aboard King Air 200 airplanes. Only eight FAA Service Difficulty Reports regarding King Air 200 inverters were submitted during a period of almost 15 years, and none of the eight reports involved a dual inverter failure. The Safety Board notes that, in October 1990, both inverters aboard the accident airplane were reported as inoperative for several minutes, but the cause of the problem was found to be a failed relay (which was then replaced) and not the failure of both inverters. Also, the maintenance records for the accident airplane did not indicate a systemic problem with either inverter. In addition, the internal fuses from both inverters were found broken but not melted or burned, which indicated that the inverters had not shorted.

Third, the King Air 200 electrical system schematic indicates that, if at least one of the inverters is operational, no a.c. power is present at the volt/frequency meter, and d.c. power is available to the inverters, then one of three components—the inverter selector switch, the inverter select relay, or the avionics inverter select relay—could produce an a.c. power electrical system failure (see figure 2). Thus, all three components are potential sources of single-point failures in the electrical system. None of these items was recovered from the wreckage.

Fourth, wiring failures, shorts, or opens are possible reasons for the loss of a.c. power.

The Safety Board cannot make a definitive determination regarding what caused the a.c. electrical system to fail. However, the Safety Board concludes that the a.c. electrical failure was a contributing factor to this accident but was not a causal factor because non-a.c.-powered instrumentation remained available for the duration of the flight for the pilot to use to safely fly and land the airplane.[50]

---

[50] The Safety Board is not making any recommendations in this report regarding the a.c. electrical failure aboard the airplane because the FAA already requires pilots to be trained to fly and land airplanes using standby flight instruments.

2.5 Oklahoma State University's Team Travel Policies

OSU's former air transportation policy was not causal to the accident. In fact, the policy was not likely different from those in place at other universities of the same size as OSU. However, even though the university's athletic department knew the accident pilot, the Flight Department had no records on file regarding him, the second pilot, or the accident airplane, as required. Also, because the accident flight was a donated flight, it was not coordinated with the Flight Department Manager, as were charter flights and flights involving university airplanes. Thus, the Safety Board concludes that OSU did not provide any significant oversight for the accident flight.

The Safety Board investigated another accident involving a university athletic team in which no significant oversight occurred. On October 2, 1970, a Martin 404, N464M, was transporting members of the Wichita State University football team from Wichita, Kansas, to Logan, Utah. After a refueling stop in Denver, the flight crew deviated from the flight plan and proceeded via a "scenic" route with mountains on both sides of the flightpath. Subsequently, the airplane crashed into the base of a mountain 8 miles west of Silver Plume, Colorado. The captain, flight attendant, and 28 passengers were killed; the first officer and 10 passengers were injured; and the airplane was destroyed by impact forces and a postcrash fire.

The Safety Board found that none of the parties involved with the flight (the owner of the airplane, the company that provided the pilots and other services, or the lessee) accepted responsibility concerning who was the operator of the flight and was thus responsible for its safe conduct.[51] The Board indicated that, if the parties denied after the accident that they were responsible for the safe conduct of the flight, it was likely that they would not have acknowledged such responsibility at the time of the flight. The Board also indicated that numerous deficiencies, unsafe practices, and deviations from regulations occurred during the flight and that the management required for a safe operation appears to have been absent, which was a "significant" factor in this accident.[52]

The Safety Board is concerned that colleges and universities may not be providing adequate oversight for athletic team travel. OSU's revised team travel policy, issued on April 22, 2002, is a comprehensive travel management system that promotes safe university-sponsored team travel and provides the necessary oversight to ensure that transportation services are carried out in accordance with the provisions of the revised policy. For example, in addition to the oversight provided by the university's athletic director, athletic staff, and coaches, OSU will retain an aviation consultant with "expertise

---

[51] The Jack Richards Aircraft Company, Inc., which owned the airplane, and Golden Eagle Aviation, Inc., which provided the pilots and other services, contended that Wichita State University was the operator. Wichita State's position was that it had merely chartered air service and thus was not the operator. The FAA's position was that Golden Eagle Aviation was the operator. The Safety Board indicated that, for purposes of the report, it was not necessary to determine which party was the official operator of the flight but that this issue needed to be fully resolved separate from the report.

[52] For more information, see National Transportation Safety Board, *Martin 404, N464M, 8 Statute Miles West of Silver Plume, Colorado, October 2, 1970,* Aircraft Accident Report NTSB/AAR-71-04 (Washington, DC: NTSB, 1971).

in operations, safety and certification." Among other things, the aviation consultant will evaluate the certifications and safety records of charter air carriers, time-share aircraft, and other aircraft and will have the final authority for approving a firm or an aircraft for the purposes of the policy.

Also, OSU's revised team travel policy provides a greater margin of safety for air transportation compared with the university's former air transportation policy, as demonstrated by the following examples:

- OSU's former air transportation policy indicated that, if the weather or the length of a trip were such that the pilot thought a copilot was necessary for the safe completion of the flight, the pilot would have the authority to dispatch a copilot for that purpose. As a result, some donated flights and possibly some charter flights were allowed to operate with one pilot (depending on whether the airplane was certified for single-pilot operation). In fact, a friend of the accident pilot stated, in a postaccident interview, that the pilot often flew for OSU as a single pilot because the athletic staff wanted to use all of the seats. The revised team travel policy, however, requires two pilots for all OSU air travel involving student athletes.

- The only mention in the former air transportation policy regarding pilot requirements are those for the OSU Flight Department's Cessna 421B and the other multiengine aircraft to which OSU had access. The former policy indicated that these airplanes were to be flown only by pilots from the OSU Flight Department or by qualified pilots hired by the Flight Department Manager. The pilots were required to have a commercial pilot's license; certification for single-engine, multiengine, and instrument flying; and a minimum of 2,500 hours as pilot-in-command, at least 500 of which were to have been in a multiengine airplane. The revised team travel policy requires captains and copilots to meet multiple requirements, some of which are more stringent than those required by the FAA.[53]

- The former air transportation policy indicated that university airplanes could be operated during day or night and in visual flight rules or IFR conditions. The former policy also indicated that the judgment of a pilot would always prevail regarding whether flight conditions were safe for takeoff or continuation of a flight. The revised team travel policy indicates that all flights are to be operated on an IFR flight plan and that aircraft may not depart into forecast hazardous weather conditions, including severe icing, thunderstorms,

---

[53] According to the policy, a captain is required to be employed as a full-time pilot and have an airline transport pilot rating with a current first-class medical certificate; a type rating in the airplane to be used for team travel; training in the airplane type within the past 12 months; at least 2,000 hours total flying time, including 200 hours in the airplane type to be used and 20 hours in the past 90 days in the airplane type to be used; and three instrument approaches and three night landings in the past 90 days. The policy also requires a copilot to have multiengine and instrument ratings and a current second-class medical certificate; training in the airplane type within the past 12 months; at least 1,500 hours total flying time, including 100 hours in the airplane type to be used and 10 hours in the past 90 days in the airplane type to be used; and three instrument approaches and three night landings in the past 90 days.

or severe turbulence or windshear. Also, the revised policy indicates that passengers cannot enter the cockpit or distract the pilots when an aircraft is below 10,000 feet on takeoff or landing operations and that aircraft used for team travel cannot be piloted by a team member.

- No specific restrictions on athletic team travel were provided in the former air transportation policy. The revised team travel policy indicates that other aircraft, including donated aircraft, are an acceptable means of travel for coaches and professional athletic department staff but that student athletes and teams are generally not permitted to travel on such aircraft.[54] (Students are allowed to travel on commercial, charter, and time-share aircraft.) Coaches, professional athletic department staff, and student athletes traveling under special circumstances can decline travel on other aircraft, in which case accommodating transportation (within the framework of the policy) will be provided. Unlike the former policy, specific requirements must now be met for other aircraft, including that the aircraft are powered by two or more turbine engines and are certified for flight into known icing conditions.

- The former air transportation policy did not mention any provisions regarding airplane maintenance. The revised team travel policy indicates that inspection and maintenance must be performed by an appropriately rated FAA-certified repair station, the manufacturer, or a manufacturer-authorized service center. The revised policy further indicates that maintenance personnel must be appropriately rated and must have been trained within the previous 5 years to maintain the aircraft type to be used.

On June 18, 2002, OSU's Vice President of Business and External Relations, along with two colleagues, presented the university's revised team travel policy to the National Association of Collegiate Athletic Directors at a convention in Dallas, Texas. The Safety Board notes that this presentation was a positive initial step to inform college and university athletic directors and senior athletic administrators of OSU's comprehensive team travel policy. However, athletic directors and senior athletic administrators who are not members of the association, as well as senior administrators outside of athletic departments, also need to be made aware of OSU's revised policy. The adoption of a comprehensive team travel policy, such as the one developed by OSU, would ensure the necessary oversight for athletic team and other school-sponsored travel and would provide an extra margin of safety for students, faculty, and staff.

The Safety Board recognizes that not all colleges and universities have athletic programs the size of the OSU program and that some schools do not even have an athletic program. However, the guidance outlined in OSU's revised team travel policy can be adapted to smaller-scale athletic programs and to club and academic travel, especially because the policy addresses specific requirements for travel by automobiles and minivans, 12- and 15-passenger vans, buses, and mini-buses.[55] (As stated earlier, OSU's

---

[54] The revised team travel policy indicates that, "in special circumstances, if three or fewer athletes are needed for official business of the department, such student athletes may accompany a coach on other aircraft if written parental/guardian consent has been received for any athlete less than 21 years of age."

policy indicates that 15-passenger vans can transport no more than 10 passengers and equipment. According to the Board's October 2002 safety report, research from the National Highway Traffic Safety Administration indicated that, in 2001, 15-passenger vans with 10 or more occupants were three times more likely to be involved in a rollover accident than those vans with fewer than 10 occupants.[56] The Board is concerned that 15-passenger vans carrying 10 occupants and athletic equipment may not have the same margin of safety from rollovers as vans carrying fewer than 10 occupants and no equipment because the weight and position of the equipment would cause the van's center of gravity to move rearward and upward.)

The Safety Board also recognizes that not all colleges and universities have budgets to support the specific requirements described in the revised OSU team travel policy. However, the Safety Board concludes that colleges and universities would benefit from reviewing a model policy based on OSU's postaccident team travel policy and then implementing a travel policy that is commensurate with the institution's travel needs. Therefore, the Safety Board believes that the National Collegiate Athletic Association, the National Association of Intercollegiate Athletics, and the American Council on Education should review OSU's postaccident team travel policy and develop, either independently or jointly, a model policy for member institutions to use in creating a travel policy or strengthening an existing travel policy.

---

[55] OSU is not the only university to develop a written driving policy after an accident. On February 10, 2000, a 1999 Ford E-350 XLT 15-passenger van was transporting a track coach, an athletic trainer, and eight student athletes from Prairie View A&M University, near Hempstead, Texas, to a men's indoor track meet at the University of Arkansas at Pine Bluff. When the van was on Texas State Highway 43 near Karnack, Texas (a two-lane highway), the van driver (a student athlete) tried to pass a Jeep Cherokee but then decided to reverse this passing action. The van subsequently went out of control and rolled over. Four of the van occupants were killed, and six were seriously injured. The Safety Board determined that a contributing factor to this accident was Prairie View's lack of oversight regarding the transportation of student athletes.

At the time of the accident, Prairie View's only written driving policy was a provision in its Athletic Policies & Procedures manual requiring that designated speed laws be obeyed when official vehicles were used for team functions. In June 2001, the Texas legislature passed a bill requiring that, by August 2002, all public institutions of higher education have a travel policy addressing fatigue, use of seatbelts, passenger capacity, and qualifications and training of drivers who operate a particular mode of transportation. In December 2001, Prairie View adopted a vehicle safety policy that conforms to the State requirements.

[56] For more information, see National Transportation Safety Board, *Evaluating the Rollover Propensity of 15-Passenger Vans,* Safety Report NTSB/SR-02-03 (Washington, DC: NTSB, 2002).

3. Conclusions

3.1 Findings

1. The pilot was properly certificated and qualified under Federal regulations. No evidence indicates any preexisting medical or behavioral conditions that might have adversely affected the pilot's performance during the accident flight.

2. The second pilot was properly certificated and qualified under Federal regulations. The second pilot was not a required flight crewmember because the airplane was certified for single-pilot operation under 14 *Code of Federal Regulations* (CFR) Part 91. Even if the flight had been operated under 14 CFR Part 135, the second pilot would still not have been a required crewmember; the airplane was certified for single-pilot operation under Part 135 in instrument flight rules conditions because a three-axis autopilot was installed and operating. Because the flight was conducted with two qualified pilots and an operational autopilot and thus exceeded Part 135 requirements, the circumstances of this accident would not have been any different if the pilot had operated the flight under Part 135 rather than Part 91.

3. The accident airplane was properly certified, equipped, and maintained in accordance with Federal regulations. The recovered components showed no evidence of any preexisting structural, engine, or system failures.

4. Icing was not a factor in this accident.

5. No evidence of a cabin pressurization problem was found.

6. This accident was not survivable for any of the airplane occupants because they were subjected to impact forces that exceeded the limits of human tolerance.

7. The physical evidence recovered from the wreckage site and the recorded radar data indicate that a complete loss of a.c. electrical power occurred aboard the airplane.

8. The pilot would have had salient cues to identify the a.c. electrical power failure.

9. The pilot did not appropriately manage the workload associated with troubleshooting the loss of a.c. electrical power with the need to establish and maintain positive control of the airplane.

10. The airplane's estimated flightpath in the final 2 minutes of flight was consistent with a graveyard spiral resulting from pilot spatial disorientation.

11. The airplane's angle at the time of impact indicated that the pilot attempted to arrest the descent in the final portion of the flight, possibly in response to obtaining visual references of the ground after emerging from the lowest layer of clouds.

12. The in-flight breakup occurred because the aerodynamic loading during the pilot's pull-up maneuver was great enough to overload the horizontal stabilizer downward and the right outboard wing section was sufficiently loaded upward to sustain a permanent bend in the spar.

13. The a.c. electrical failure was a contributing factor to this accident but was not a causal factor because non-a.c.-powered instrumentation remained available for the duration of the flight for the pilot to use to safely fly and land the airplane.

14. Oklahoma State University did not provide any significant oversight for the accident flight.

15. Colleges and universities would benefit from reviewing a model policy based on Oklahoma State University's postaccident team travel policy and then implementing a travel policy that is commensurate with the institution's travel needs.

3.2 Probable Cause

The National Transportation Safety Board determines that the probable cause of this accident was the pilot's spatial disorientation resulting from his failure to maintain positive manual control of the airplane with the available flight instrumentation. Contributing to the cause of the accident was the loss of a.c. electrical power during instrument meteorological conditions.

4.   Recommendation

As a result of the investigation of this accident, the National Transportation Safety Board makes the following recommendation to the National Collegiate Athletic Association, the National Association of Intercollegiate Athletics, and the American Council on Education:

Review Oklahoma State University's postaccident team travel policy and develop, either independently or jointly, a model policy for member institutions to use in creating a travel policy or strengthening an existing travel policy. (A-03-01)

BY THE NATIONAL TRANSPORTATION SAFETY BOARD

CAROL J. CARMODY
Acting Chairman

JOHN J. GOGLIA
Member

JOHN A. HAMMERSCHMIDT
Member

GEORGE W. BLACK, JR.
Member

Adopted: January 15, 2003

5. Appendixes

Appendix A
Investigation and Hearing

Investigation

The National Transportation Safety Board was initially notified of this accident on January 27, 2001, about 2030 eastern standard time (1830 mountain standard time). A go-team was assembled and departed at 0500 eastern standard time on January 28, 2001, from Ronald Reagan National Airport in Washington, D.C., for Denver, Colorado. The team arrived on scene about 1040 eastern standard time (0840 mountain standard time). Accompanying the team to Strasburg was Board Member John Hammerschmidt.

The following investigative teams were formed: Aircraft Operations, Human Performance, Aircraft Structures, Aircraft Systems, Powerplants, Maintenance Records, Air Traffic Control, Meteorology, and Aircraft Performance.

Parties to the investigation were the Federal Aviation Administration, Oklahoma State University, Raytheon Aircraft Company, and Pratt & Whitney Canada Aircraft Services, Inc.

Public Hearing

No public hearing was held for this accident.

Appendix B
Oklahoma State University's Revised Team Travel Policy

TASK FORCE REPORT
OSU TEAM TRAVEL POLICY

1.01   Purpose

A. To provide a framework for safe and efficient athletic team travel for the Oklahoma State University Department of Intercollegiate Athletics.

B. To assign responsibility and accountability for enforcement.

2.01   Applicability

For purposes of this policy, athletic teams are defined as:

Baseball
Basketball, Women's and Men's
Equestrian
Football
Golf, Women's and Men's
Soccer
Softball
Tennis, Women's and Men's
Track (Indoor, Outdoor, Cross Country), Women's and Men's
Wrestling
Mascots, Spirit Squad, Student Trainers, and/or Student Mangers traveling as a part of a team
        listed above
or any other such team as may be subsequently added to the OSU Intercollegiate Athletics
        Program

3.01   Responsibility for administration

A. The OSU Director of Intercollegiate Athletics shall be responsible for overall administration of this policy and shall assign a member of the athletics staff to be responsible for compliance, oversight and necessary recordkeeping. The OSU Director of Intercollegiate Athletics or his/her designee shall provide a copy of this policy to every coach; provide training to every coach; and maintain on file in the Athletic Department a signed certificate by each coach stating the coach has read and understands this policy.

B. The OSU Director of Intercollegiate Athletics or his/her designee shall have the responsibility to verify the type of vehicle recommended for use for athletic travel is in compliance with this policy. Coaches are responsible for developing their season travel plans, to include recommended vehicle types, and gaining written approval from the appropriate associate athletic director in advance of the season or subsequent schedule change. Coaches will consider the type of travel necessary to comply with the institutional policy on missed classes. Post-season travel shall be handled according to NCAA guidelines and approved by the OSU Director of Intercollegiate Athletics or his/her designee.

C. When aircraft are used under this policy, the captain (pilot in command) shall make the final decision whether to fly. However, in no case will the pilot fly if weather conditions do not meet the standards of his/her certification. The respective head coach may always overrule the pilot if he/she concludes that it is inappropriate to fly.

D. The OSU Director of Intercollegiate Athletics or his/her designee shall review and recommend revision, as deemed appropriate to this policy annually, in accordance with institutional guidelines on policy revisions.

4.01 Accountability

Any coach or athletic staff member knowingly violating this policy will be suspended with or without pay until the OSU Director of Intercollegiate Athletics or his/her designee investigates the violation. Violations may result in disciplinary action or termination.

5.01 Supplemental Insurance

OSU will procure and maintain in effect accidental death benefits that will guarantee an amount up to $1 million, but not less than $250,000 for travel connected to athletic competition and practice [in accordance with NCAA Bylaw 16.4.1-(b) or as amended]. Coverage per person will be in addition to any other coverages for student athletes, coaches, mascots, spirit squad, student trainers, student managers, and Athletic Department members while on authorized Athletic Department business.

6.01 Types of Vehicles Used for Team Travel and Requirements for Operation

General Requirement: Coaches, assistant coaches, student trainers, student managers, mascots and members of the spirit squad may drive vehicles used for team travel, if the specific requirements for the vehicle are met. Student athletes may not drive other athletes as a part of team travel.

The following types of vehicles shall be approved for athletic team travel under the conditions noted:

A.   Automobiles/Minivans (Specific Requirements)

1.   Drivers must be at least 21 years of age, have a valid and approved driver's license and be rested.

2.   A qualified, paid driver must be used if traveling farther than 350 miles one way, or if the trip is expected to extend later than 2:00 a.m., or overnight.

B.   Twelve and Fifteen Passenger Vans (Specific Requirements)

1.   Drivers are required to obtain a certification from an Emergency Vehicle Operator's Course in the type of vehicle they will be driving.

2.   Drivers must be at least 21 years of age, have a valid and approved driver's license and be rested.

3. For safety reasons, drivers must have a Class C(P) Commercial Driver's License whether or not required by law.

4. Drivers must submit to a health check as required by the license or, upon hiring, must pass a medical exam and pass an annual exam thereafter.

5. A qualified, paid driver must be used if traveling farther than 350 miles one way or if the trip is expected to extend later than 2:00 a.m., or overnight.

6. Only vans with a 155 inch wheelbase equipped with "E" rated radial tires, or equivalent, properly inflated will be allowed to transport teams greater than 100 miles from a point of departure. In cases when it is necessary to lease vans from a commercial vendor or when vans are provided as a courtesy, team travel is authorized even if the van does not meet the 155 inch/"E" criteria, but travel will be limited to 100 miles one way.

7. Twelve passenger vans shall be loaded with no more than eight passengers and equipment. Fifteen passenger vans shall be loaded with no more than ten passengers and equipment.

C. Buses (Specific Requirements)

1. When more than 20 passengers are part of the land travel party, a bus or mini-bus shall be used.

2. Buses may be used to transport to away venues, transport to hotels from airports, and transport from hotels to playing venues.

3. Approved buses for team transport are motor coach common carriers or institution leased, owned or operated over-the-road bus transports.

4. Drivers of buses must have a valid and approved Class B(P) Commercial Driver's License.

5. Drivers must submit to a health check as required by the license or, upon hiring, must pass a medical exam and pass an annual exam thereafter.

D. Mini-buses (defined as 20 – 30 passenger transports) (Specific Requirements)

1. When more than 20 passengers are part of the land travel party, a bus or mini-bus shall be used.

2. Acceptable mini-buses shall be institution owned or commercially owned.

3. Driver must have a valid and approved Class B(P) Commercial Drivers License to operate a mini-bus for purposes of this policy.

4. Drivers must submit to a health check as required by the license or, upon hiring, must pass a medical exam and pass an annual exam thereafter.

E.   Air Transportation

Commercial air carriers, charter, time-share and other aircraft may be used for the purposes stated and are subject to the provisions below:

1. Commercial Airlines

    Commercial airlines are an acceptable means of travel for athletic teams. Tickets must be procured under the travel guidelines established by the State of Oklahoma.

2. Use of Aviation Consultant

    All air travel, except the use of commercial air carriers, shall be subject to the review of the institution's aviation consultant.

    The University will, through competitive proposals, retain an aviation consultant. Such individual or firm must have expertise in operations, safety and certification for the purpose of evaluating the certifications and safety records, of charter air carriers, time-share and other aircraft and assure pilot certifications are in keeping with this policy. The aviation consultant will evaluate and assure insurance coverage consistent with this policy.

    Prior to flying, the institutional aviation consultant must assure that charter companies, time-share companies, other aircraft and all pilots flying other aircraft meet the requirements of this policy. The aviation consultant shall maintain a qualified list of time-share and other aircraft for possible use.

    The institutional aviation consultant shall have final approving authority for approving a firm/aircraft for purposes of this policy.

3. General Requirements for Charter, Time-Share, and Other Aircraft

    a) Insurance

    Aircraft owners/operators shall furnish proof of insurance in advance. Liability insurance should be at least $25 million for light turboprop aircraft, $50 million for light jet aircraft, and a minimum of $3 million per seat for Commercial airlines. Given the volatility in the insurance market, it may not always be possible to achieve these minimum coverages in the marketplace. If it becomes necessary to establish limits in keeping with current industry standards, it shall be the responsibility of the University's aviation consultant to recommend acceptable limits.

b) Pilots

Two pilots will be required for all OSU travel involving student athletes. Pilots for small aircraft (maximum gross weight of 12,500 lbs or less), whether charter, time-share or other shall have, as a minimum:

b(1) Captain

- Airline Transport Pilot (ATP) rating with current first class medical.
- Type rating in aircraft to be used for team travel.
- Training in the aircraft type to be used at Flight Safety International, Simuflite Training International, or equivalent aircraft manufacturer's training within the past 12 months.
- Be employed as a full-time pilot.
- 2000 hours total flying time.
- 200 hours total flying time in the aircraft type to be used.
- 20 hours flying time in the past 90 days in the aircraft type to be used.
- Three instrument approaches and three night landings in the previous 90 days.

b(2) Copilot

- Commercial Pilot Certificate with current second class medical with multi-engine and instrument ratings.
- Training in the aircraft type to be used at Flight Safety International, Simuflite Training International, or equivalent aircraft manufacturer's training within the past 12 months.
- 1500 hours total flying time.
- 100 hours total flying time in the aircraft type to be used.
- 10 hours flying time in the past 90 days in the aircraft type to be used.
- Three instrument approaches and three night landings in the previous 90 days.

c) Maintenance

c(1) Inspection and maintenance must be performed by an appropriately rated FAA certified repair station, the manufacturer or a manufacturer authorized service center (no Aircraft and Powerplant Mechanic signoffs).

c(2) Maintenance personnel (or at least the person signing the log books) must be appropriately rated and be trained to maintain the aircraft type to be used by either Flight Safety International or Simuflite Training International within the previous five years.

c(3) Charter aircraft used according to this policy must be maintained under the appropriate FAA operations specifications.

d) Operation

d(1) On all light turboprop and light jet aircraft, weight and balance computations using average passenger weights are prohibited. A weight and balance form must be completed for each flight using actual weight figures for passengers (no quick weight and balance using normal passenger weights).

d(2) No over-weight or out of center of gravity operation shall be allowed.

d(3) No aircraft may depart into forecast hazardous weather conditions, such as severe icing, thunderstorms or severe turbulence or wind shear.

d(4) No circling instrument approaches shall be authorized with ceilings less than 1,000 feet and at least three miles visibility.

d(5) All flights shall be conducted on an instrument flight plan.

d(6) No passengers may enter the cockpit or distract pilots when the aircraft is below 10,000 feet on takeoff or landing operations.

d(7) Aircraft should be hangered whenever possible during inclement weather.

d(8) No aircraft used for team transportation may be piloted by a team member.

d(9) All flight operations must be conducted in accordance with all relevant FAA regulations or insurance requirements, whichever is more strict.

4.   Charter Services (Specific Requirements)

a) All charter services procured shall be subject to the involvement of the OSU Purchasing Department.

b) Every charter company used must have and demonstrate evidence of a current air carrier certificate under FAA Part 135 or 121.

c) The OSU institutional aviation consultant shall assure the OSU Director of Intercollegiate Athletics or his/her designee that written verification has been received for all charter flights from the FAA Flight Standards District Office (FSDO) that an Air Carrier Operating Certificate has been filed and is being maintained in good standing.

5.   Time-share aircraft is authorized if an individual sport budget is sufficient to pay any applicable and operational costs and if any of the conditions below apply:

a) Time is available to the Athletic Department in the time-share pool, either owned by the University, corporate or an individual ownership.

b) Such use will facilitate travel and keep student athletes from missing excessive class time.

c) It will facilitate the recruiting image or funding efforts of the department.

d) Commercial or charter services cannot otherwise accommodate the necessary schedule.

6. Other Aircraft (Specific Requirements)

Other aircraft are an acceptable means of travel for coaches and professional athletic department staff, based on personal election, provided all requirements in Section 6.01 E 3 "General Requirements for Charter, Time-Share and Other Aircraft" have been met and the following specific requirements are met. Student athletes and teams shall not be permitted to travel on such other aircraft, except that in special circumstances if three or fewer athletes are needed for official business of the department, such student athletes may accompany a coach on other aircraft if written parental/guardian consent has been received for any athlete less than 21 years of age. Coaches, professional athletic department staff or student athletes may decline to travel on such other aircraft, in which case accommodating transportation (within the framework of this policy) will be provided.

a) Other Aircraft

a(1) The aircraft are powered by two or more turbine engines.

a(2) The aircraft are certified for flight into known icing conditions.

a(3) The aircraft otherwise meets all FAA and insurance requirements of OSU's travel policy (whichever are most strict).

b) Other Aircraft Approval

The institutional aviation consultant must approve in writing the use of aircraft prior to travel (See Section 6.01 E 2).

c) Other Aircraft Documentation

Before any aircraft is approved for use, the owner/operator shall provide and the institutional aviation consultant shall evaluate and approve in writing the compliance of the following:

c(1) Proof of insurance with required minimums.

c(2) Documentation showing the maintenance plan under which the aircraft operates complies with the requirements of this policy.

c(3) Pilot experience and training documents showing qualifications meeting or ex the requirements of this policy.

c(4) Documents showing the aircraft payload capabilities for use in trip planning.

www.ingramcontent.com/pod-product-compliance
Lightning Source LLC
Chambersburg PA
CBHW080909290526
45795CB00007BA/2474